A **SAGE** HUMAN SERVICES GUIDE **44**

PURCHASE OF SERVICE CONTRACTING

Peter M. KETTNER
Lawrence L. MARTIN

*Published in cooperation with the University of
Michigan School of Social Work*

SAGE PUBLICATIONS
Newbury Park   Beverly Hills   London   New Delhi

For information address:

SAGE Publications, Inc.
2111 West Hillcrest Drive
Newbury Park, California 91320

SAGE Publications Inc.
275 South Beverly Drive
Beverly Hills
California 90212

SAGE Publications Ltd.
28 Banner Street
London EC1Y 8QE
England

SAGE PUBLICATIONS India Pvt. Ltd.
M-32 Market
Greater Kailash I
New Delhi 110 048 India

Printed in the United States of America

Library of Congress Cataloging-in-Publication Data

Kettner, Peter M., 1936-
    Purchase of service contracting

    (Sage human services guides ; v. 44)
      1. Social service--United States--Contracting out.
I. Martin, Lawrence L.   II. Title.   III. Series.
HV41.K48 1986   350.84′0973   86-1928
ISBN 0-8039-2630-8 (pbk.)

Contents

Preface

Pucka

Purchase of service contracting (POSC) has, in many significant ways, changed the way human services are structured and delivered in this country. It is a rare practitioner that is not affect in some way by POSC. Most private agencies now have contracts with the government. Many public social service employees have some responsibility for contracts. Yet very few human service professionals have had any formal education or training in the philosophy, concepts, issues, and technology of POSC.

This lack of training is evident in practice. Studies have revealed chaotic and inconsistent practices as well as shifting philosophies. The time has come, we believe, for practitioners to become grounded in a knowledge and skill base developed from years of experience and research in POSC. This book attempts to present at least a skeleton of a conceptual/theoretical framework for POSC system design and practice. These theoretical underpinnings, we hope, can lead to more study and ever-improving POSC practice.

Our intent in writing this volume is to be descriptive, explanatory, and prescriptive, all at the same time. Through an exhaustive review of the POSC literature, including many government documents, we have distilled the basic components and practices of a complete POSC system. Through an analysis of several studies of state experiences with POSC, we have attempted to create a frame of reference for decision making in POSC. Through a step-by-step explanation of the process, we have described how one can create a soundly designed and well run POSC system.

We believe the book will be useful to a variety of audiences, including the following:

- professors of social work and public administration whose academic interests and teaching assignments are in human services policy, planning, and administration;

- students preparing for careers in human services policy, planning, and administration;
- professionals working in private human service agencies that are involved, or are considering involvement, as contractors;
- all levels of administrators in state, county, and municipal human service agencies; and
- legislators, advocates, or concerned citizens who are interested in gaining a better understanding of the POSC process in human services.

In any effort like this we are, of course, grateful for the help and support of a number of people. To the many students and trainees who have helped shape our thinking and our understanding, we express our thanks. To the many scholars who have provided the conceptual and empirical base from which we have drawn, we extend our appreciation. To readers of early drafts—Joseph Warnas, Ernest Workman, and Judy Kettner—we owe a debt of gratitude for thoughtful comments and insights. To Armand Lauffer we express our thanks for his vision and clarity in keeping the book on track, and to Laura Orr and Betty Wood we extend our warmest expression of appreciation for being so pleasant in typing this volume in spite of our many unreasonable requests.

We're aware that there is still a general perception that POSC involves simply a set of techniques and relatively minor policy issues. We hope this volume will contribute to changing those ideas and to bringing a conceptually sound, empirically based, and steadily improving POSC system to states, counties, and municipalities. To the many practitioners who are committed to making that happen, we dedicate this book.

—Peter M. Kettner
Lawrence L. Martin

Part I

CONCEPTS AND ISSUES IN PURCHASE OF SERVICE CONTRACTING

Chapter 1

WHAT IS A CONTRACT?

OBJECTIVES

By the end of this chapter the reader should be able to:

- Define the following key concepts:
    - Contract
    - Grant and grant-in-aid
    - Cooperative agreement
    - Offer
    - Acceptance
    - Consideration
    - Legal capacity
    - Parole evidence rule
    - Ultra vires
- Discuss or explain the following:
    - The differences between procurement and assistance
    - The importance of the Federal Grant and Cooperative Agreement Act and the American Bar Association's Model Procurement codes for state, county, and municipal governments
    - The differing status of clients under grants-in-aid and contracts

---

Over the past two decades human service agencies have experienced major changes in their budgeting and funding practices. An example of a family and children's service agency will illustrate some of these changes.

As the 1960s began, Springdale Family and Children's Services received most of its funding from two sources—the United Way and a charity drive sponsored by a religious denomination, because the agency was church affiliated. Client fees contributed minor support. Funding from the United Way and the church was stable and predictable. Everyone understood that fund-raising goals for each year would take inflation into consideration and a steady increase each year could be expected.

Toward the end of the 1960s, the agency board attempted to respond with a renewed sense of awareness to the needs of the poor and oppressed by adding a number of new programs. The federal government made funds available to expand services to reach out to ethnic minority families with incomes below the poverty line. New staff—including many paraprofessionals and economically disadvantaged people—were hired. These programs grew steadily though the early 1970s, assuming a major role in overall agency operation.

By this time United Way support accounted for only a fraction of the total budget, and church contributions had almost disappeared. The bulk of the agency budget was now made up of public funds.

In the mid-1970s the government began to make many demands in return for its funding. Money was systematically channeled through the state, and the agency was required to develop an annual proposal, detailing problems to be addressed, stating objectives, developing action plans, and calculating unit costs. They were even asked to sign a contract stating that they would perform services as specified in the contract document. The agency executive director and supervisory staff found these demands extremely frustrating—"just useless paperwork," they said. But they were, in a sense, trapped. The agency had drifted significantly from its ties to the church. The United Way could not increase its support because of the many demands placed on its resources. Springdale Family and Children's Services had become in a sense a quasi-public agency.

We suspect that this experience is not unique. We hope that in the following pages, human service agency personnel will find some answers that will help them understand the funding context in which they find themselves, and the many technicalities associated with the use of government funding (and their rationale), and help them be able to operate in a Purchase of Service Contracting (POSC) system in a knowledgeable, professional, and confident manner.

FROM GRANTS TO CONTRACTS

Many people who remember the days when the predominant method of federal funding in human services was the grant see the contract as being basically the same type of arrangement under a different name. In practice and in law this is not the case. A contract is an agreement enforceable by law. It contains some understandings about exchange between two parties. These understandings are different in a number of ways from a grant. Most important, a contract implies *procurement* or *purchase* whereas a grant implies *assistance*. In this chapter the differences between, and the appropriate uses of, the POSC approach and the grants-in-aid approach will be discussed. The elements of contract formation will be identified, and selected general contract law terms will be introduced and defined.

DISTINGUISHING PROCUREMENT AND
ASSISTANCE RELATIONSHIPS

The appropriate uses of the POSC approach and the grants-in-aid approach have not always been as clearly defined as they are today. In the past, some government human services agencies used both grants and contracts to fund exactly the same services. Many utilized both POSC and grants-in-aid interchangeably.

This blurring of distinctions eventually led to major problems for both government and those private human services agencies that were recipients of contracts or grants. For example, the responsibilities and the rights of both sets of agencies were often in dispute because the responsibilities and rights of parties are different under POSC and grants-in-aid. Determining the proper application of federal and state laws was also difficult because some laws apply only to contracts and others only to grants-in-aid. The problems associated with attempting to sort out POSC from grants-in-aid became particularly troublesome and costly for the federal government. Federal legislation was eventually passed to resolve these issues.

At the joint urging of the Congress and the Federal Office of Management and Budget (OMB), the Federal Commission on Government Procurement undertook the task of developing criteria for differentiating between the appropriate uses of contracts and grants-in-aid. The Commission's recommendations were translated into law in the form of the *Federal Grant & Cooperative Agreement Act of 1977*.

The Act states that the use of contracts is to be restricted solely to procurement relationships. Grants-in-aid, together with cooperative agreements—a newly created type of arrangement—are to be used for assistance relationships. The distinction between procurement and assistance relationships is to be determined by the public purposes for which federal funds are to be expended.

As Figure 1.1 illustrates, when a government contracting agency contemplates expending funds to secure (purchase) services for its own purposes, a procurement relationship is deemed to exist and a contract is required. When a government contracting agency contemplates expending funds to assist an agency in discharging its own responsibilities, an assistance relationship is deemed to exist and either grants-in-aid or cooperative agreements are required.

Whether grants-in-aid or cooperative agreements are used for assistance relationships is dependent upon the degree of involvement, if any, that a government contracting agency wishes to have in determining how the recipient of funds operates its program or provides its services. When direct involvement on the part of a federal agency is contemplated, the Federal Grant & Cooperative Agreement Act requires that cooperative agreements be used. When no direct involvement is contemplated, grants-in-aid are to be used. For example, the U.S. Department of Health and Human Services may want to support two projects in permanency planning for foster care. One project may be proceeding satisfactorily and the Department may want to continue it exactly as is. This project would be funded through a grant-in-aid. The second project may be experiencing some difficulty in data collection, but is still seen as a good project worthy of continued support. In this instance they would use a cooperative agreement and would send in staff members to help correct the problems.

Similar efforts to distinguish between procurement and assistance relationships are also taking place at the state and local levels. A few years ago the American Bar Association developed model procurement codes for state, county, and municipal governments (American Bar Association, 1981). These model codes attempt, in part, to accomplish for state and local governments what the Federal Grant & Cooperative Agreement Act did for the federal government. As of this writing twelve states have adopted all or significant portions of the model procurement code and several others have legislation pending.

The distinction between procurement and assistance is an extremely important one because it establishes the basis for the relationship

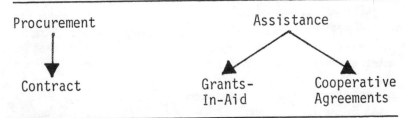

Figure 1.1: Appropriate uses of contract, grants-in-aid, and cooperative agreements.

between funder and provider. Under the POSC approach, the contractor is simply a provider of service. The clients being served are clients of the state, county, or municipal government contracting agency. The government agency is ultimately responsible for their health and welfare even though services are provided by another agency. Thus the government contracting agency has an absolute right to access or possess any and all relevant client, services, or financial information. Conversely, when a government agency uses the grants-in-aid approach, the clients being served are deemed to be clients of the provider agency. Ownership of client, services, and financial information resides with the provider agency.

As a result of the Federal Grant & Cooperative Agreement Act and the American Bar Association's model procurement codes, the distinctions between procurement and assistance and the appropriate uses of POSC contracts, grants-in-aid, and cooperative agreements are becoming increasingly standardized nationally and can be summarized under three concepts: purchaser, partner, and patron, as indicated below.

The Appropriate Uses Of POSC Contracts, Grants-in-Aid And Cooperative Agreements

- **Purchaser** The government agency is a *purchaser* of services from private agencies through the use of *contracts.*
- **Partner** The government agency is a *partner* with private agencies sharing in decision making and providing funds through *cooperative agreements.*
- **Patron** The government agency is a *patron* supporting the efforts of private agencies through the use of *grants-in-aid.*

From this point forward, we shall be dealing only with the procurement of human services by government contracting agencies using POSC. Nothing more will be said either in this chapter or in the remainder of this book about grants-in-aid or cooperative agreements.[1]

THE ELEMENTS OF CONTRACT FORMATION

A contract is essentially a legal concept. Although many definitions of the term exist, the one most frequently used comes from a group of research books that are known collectively as the "Restatement of Contracts":

Definition of Contract

A promise or set of promises for breach of which the law gives a remedy or the performance of which the law in some way recognizes a duty. (Office of Federal Procurement Policy, 1979)

In other words, a contract is an agreement that the law will enforce. This distinction is important in that all contracts are agreements but not all agreements are contracts. "Agreement" is a much broader term than "contract" and encompasses those promises that the law will enforce as well as those the law will not enforce. Two or more parties may make an agreement to do something but a contract has not necessarily been formed. For example, two human services administrators may agree to cochair a committee, but the law does not recognize that any contractual obligation has been created. The types of agreements that our legal system enforce are those that are deemed to have sufficient economic or social importance.

For a contract to come into being certain requirements, known as the elements of contract formation, must be satisfied. There are six elements of contract formation:

Elements of Contract Formation

- Offer
- Acceptance
- Consideration
- Legal Capacity of the Parties
- Legal Subject Matter
- Written Document (if required by law)

The absence of any one of these six elements is sufficient by itself to preclude a contract from being formed.

ELEMENT 1: OFFER

The creation of a contract begins when one party makes an offer to another party. An offer can be defined as a proposal made by the offeror to the offeree that is meant to create a legal relationship. Put more simply, an offer is a proposal that a contract be formed. An offer must be stated in sufficiently definite and certain terms so that the specific nature of the offer can be determined by the offeree. A letter stating, "We would be interested in expanding our services to people residing in the northeast sector of the county," does not constitute an offer because it does not include definite and certain terms. A complete proposal with detailed plans for service delivery and communication of a willingness to serve that population in exchange for funding would constitute an offer. The critical components of an offer include the following: (1) a clear intent to contract (2) stated in definite and certain terms and (3) communicated to the offeree.

ELEMENT 2: ACCEPTANCE

Acceptance usually means simply saying "yes" to the terms and conditions of the offer. As a general rule, an offer must be accepted unequivocally. Any deviation from the exact nature of the offer constitutes a counteroffer. In POSC, a great deal of counteroffering or negotiation may take place. In such situations, acceptance comes about only when the government contracting agency and the prospective contractor have reached a mutually satisfactory agreement to which both parties say "yes."

ELEMENT 3: CONSIDERATION

"Consideration" is the legal term used to describe the promises that are mutually exchanged by the contracting parties. Consideration in POSC usually takes the form of (1) the potential contractor promising to provide a service in accordance with the requirements set out by the government contracting agency, and (2) the government contracting agency promising to pay or reimburse the prospective contractor some agreed upon amount of money. The requirements utilized by the government contracting agency (called the "work statement" and covered in a later chapter) must be as precise as possible in order for the potential contractor to understand exactly what is promised. Poorly written work statements with vaguely defined expectations usually form the basis of a troublesome contractual relationship.

ELEMENT 4: LEGAL CAPACITY OF THE PARTIES

The parties to any proposed contract must have the legal capacity to bind themselves in a contractual relationship. Certain classes or persons (e.g., minors) in our society may be deemed to lack legal capacity in certain instances. Lack of legal capacity can also arise when nonprofit corporations are involved. From time-to-time, a nonprofit corporation may mistakenly attempt to enter into a contract that is not in keeping with its intended purposes or that exceeds the powers granted under its corporate charter or articles of incorporation. For example, a nonprofit corporation organized to provide services to the elderly might attempt to secure a contract to provide children's services. A corporation action of this nature is said to be *ultra vires* and can create legal complications for a government contracting agency. A necessary and important step in the procurement process is establishing the legal capacity of potential contractors.

ELEMENT 5: LEGAL SUBJECT MATTER

The right to contract is not absolute. Certain types of agreements are denied the status of contracts because their subject matter violates federal or state laws. Any agreement that involves a criminal or illegal act will not be afforded the status of a contract. In some states the law requires that child protective services be provided by state employees. Any agreement for child protective services with a private agency would be in violation of state law and therefore would not be a legal contract.

ELEMENT 6: A WRITTEN DOCUMENT (IF REQUIRED BY LAW)

In some cases there is also a requirement that the understanding of the contracting parties must be reduced to writing. At one time, the old Title XX federal regulations did permit state human services agencies to utilize oral POSC contracts in some situations. Oral POSC contracts should, however, be avoided at all costs for they are inherently flawed. The flaw is the obvious absence of any objective evidence (i.e., a writing) that sets forth the previous terms to which the government contracting agency and the contractor have agreed. There is an old saying, "An oral contract isn't worth the paper it's written on."

When a contract is reduced to writing the *parole evidence rule* comes into being. It states that when the parties to a contract have reduced their understanding to writing, the writing is considered to be the final and complete understanding of the parties and no other oral understandings are deemed to exist. If the parties to a contract agree orally to some understanding during negotiations, but the understanding is left out of the final written contract, the parties may not be bound by the understanding. Errors of this nature can, however, be corrected later by a formal written contract amendment, provided the parties all agree to the amendment. A contract amendment is essentially a new contract, the terms of which modify an existing contract.

SUMMARY

- Although the terms "grant" and "contract" have often been used interchangeably in the past, they represent two clearly different relationships.
- Grants are used when a funding source elects to assist an organization or program to continue or to enhance its own efforts.
- Contracts are used when the funding source chooses to purchase a service (rather than deliver it directly) for clients who are entitled to services from the funding source.
- The elements of contract formation are as follows: offer, acceptance, consideration, legal capacity of the parties, legal subject matter, and a written document (if required by law).

NOTE

1. For more information on grants and grantsmanship, see Lauffer (1984).

Chapter 2

PURCHASE OF SERVICE CONTRACTING (POSC) FOR HUMAN SERVICES
A Historical and Theoretical Context

OBJECTIVES

By the end of this chapter the reader should be able to:

- Define the following key concepts:
    - Purchase of service contracting (POSC)
    - Government contracting agency
    - Contractor
    - Direct delivery
    - Purchase of service
    - Fourteen decision criteria
    - Partnership model
    - Market model

- Discuss or explain the following:
    - The origins of purchase of service
    - Why the federal government promoted POSC in the 1960s
    - The reasons for the increased use of proprietary (for-profit) contractors
    - Reasons for the growth of POSC in the 1970s
    - Direct provision of service versus POSC
    - Partnership approach versus market approach
    - Criteria for developing an optimum delivery system

The dramatic increase over the past decade in the use of purchase of service contracting for the provision of human services has, for some, created the perception that purchase of service is a new concept. In actuality, the roots of the purchase of service approach can be traced back at least as far as colonial times. Furthermore, at different periods in our nation's history, purchase of service has been the preferred mode of human services delivery.

Purchase of service contracting for human services can be defined as follows:

**Definition of Purchase of Service Contracting
in Human Services**

A legally binding agreement between a *government contracting agency* (with responsibility for serving clients and the resources to serve them) and a *contractor* (with appropriate service delivery capability) in which the contractor provides care or services to clients of the government contracting agency in exchange for funds or other resources.

Several important principles are embodied in this definition. First, there is a government contracting agency that has responsibility for serving clients and has been allocated the resources to serve them. Second, there is a contractor ready, willing, and capable of providing the necessary services in exchange for funds or other resources. Third, the clients served remain the clients of the government contracting agency, even though service is provided by the contractor.

THE ORIGINS OF CONTRACTING
FOR HUMAN SERVICES

During the colonial period and beyond, the local public sector was naturally quite small and very limited in its capacity to provide services. Many services that we think of today as being provided by government were provided by the private sector. Some examples follow:

- Abused, neglected, and unattached children as well as children of families that were believed to be of questionable child-rearing capabilities would be bound over (indentured or apprenticed) by town officials to local individuals. Under this contractual type of arrangement, the town acted as broker, bringing together the child in need of food, clothing, and shelter with an individual who could benefit from the child's labor.

- Adult paupers would be farmed out or entrusted to the care of local individuals who, for an agreed upon sum of money to be paid by the town, would provide the pauper with shelter and other basic needs. If the pauper was deemed to be "able bodied," the town officials might also require, as part of the contractual arrangement, that the pauper be instructed in a useful trade.
- In 1823, it was reported that the Town of Beekman in Dutchess County had been using the contract system since 1820, paying a fixed fee of $32 per annum for each pauper over age twelve and $16 per annum for children under age twelve.
- In the Town of Amsterdam all poor were kept by a local farmer under a contract for a fixed payment of $350 per annum (Wedel, 1973, p. 3).

As towns and cities continued to grow in size and population, the individual attention required of the contract system became cumbersome and purchase of service gradually declined. Contract arrangements were eventually replaced by government-run poorhouses. Purchase of service did not, however, disappear from the scene altogether. Care for certain classes of indigents was still secured primarily from the private sector. As an example, many states maintained formal agreements with private residential institutions for the care of indigent children with handicapping conditions.

Purchase of service enjoyed a period of major revival during the late 1890s and early 1900s. This period coincided with the private charities and settlement house movements. During this time, the American Red Cross was established by Clara Barton, the Salvation Army was making its way to the United States from England, and Hull House was opened in Chicago by Jane Adams. The popular belief of the time was that private charitable groups and organizations could provide better quality human services than could government, and at a lower cost. Additionally, it was felt by many that government provision of human services stigmatized recipients, a situation that was avoided when private agencies served as an intermediary between government and recipient.

Through purchase of service arrangements large sums of local public funds began being directed to private charities for the care of public clients. Eventually purchase of service became so extensive that controversies began arising over issues of accountability for public funds and quality control over privately provided human services (sound familiar?). The controversies became so heated that in many areas countermovements were fostered to restrict the use of public funds to public agencies only. Although these countermovements were generally unsuccessful in their attempts to preclude the use of public funds by private charities, the uproar they created was such that purchase of service suffered a decline in popularity that continued for almost fifty years.

POSC IN THE 1960s

As the federal government began putting together many of the programs of the "War on Poverty" and the "Great Society" of the 1960s, the purchase of service contract was discovered. A large number of the programs initiated during this period contained explicit provisions for purchase of service contracting including the following: *The Demonstration (Model) Cities Act of 1966, The Economic Opportunity Act of 1964,* and *The Public Assistance Amendments of 1962 and 1967.* Prior to the federal initiatives of the 1960s, purchase of service had been principally motivated by a desire on the part of state and local governments to reduce the cost of services and to hold down the size of government (Nelson, 1980). The many social programs launched during the 1960s included neither of these two concerns in their objectives. Instead, the POSC concept was promoted because involvement of the private sector was adopted as a public policy priority.

The Public Assistance Amendments of 1962 and 1967—the forerunner of the federal Title XX program—created a climate that favored POSC by

- authorizing states to contract with the full range of potential contractors (other public agencies, nonprofit organizations, and for-profit firms);
- authorizing states to use "donated funds" (i.e., public and private funds turned over to state agencies) to satisfy federal matching requirements; and
- placing no limit on the amount of federal funds a state could earn.

These three conditions combined to open up theoretically unlimited federal funds for states to expand human services, often without requiring any state funding. Through the aggressive use of purchase of service contracting, state agencies created a "gold rush" of sorts on the federal treasury. Illinois, for example, succeeded in securing, in just one year (1972), federal reimbursement of $182 million (Cole, 1979). POSC activity under the Public Assistance Amendments and later under Title XX of the Social Security Act more than doubled between 1971 and 1978 (Mueller, 1978, 1980; Pacific Consultants, 1979).

POSC IN THE 1970s

The decade of the 1970s also saw the advent of the revenue-sharing approach, which gave further impetus to purchase of service contracting. Revenue sharing, originally a part of President Nixon's "New Federalism," takes essentially two forms: (1) the General Revenue Sharing program that provides federal funds to state and local governments with very few strings attached, and (2) the special revenue-sharing programs that provide federal funds to state and local government for specific types of activities. Examples of special revenue-sharing programs include the Joint Training Partnership Act of 1981, which provides federal funds for job training and retraining programs, and the Community Development Block Grant program (CDBG), otherwise known as Title I of the *Housing and Community Development Act of 1974,* which provides federal funds for community development activities.

Another important development in the history of POSC was the passage of Title XX of the Social Security Act in 1975. The advent of Title XX brought about significant changes in the manner in which most states planned and implemented their human service programs. One provision appearing in the Title XX regulations required that states spell out in their annual Title XX state plans the method of service delivery (direct, purchase-public, or purchase-private) for every service to be provided (*Code of Federal Regulations* (CRF) Chapter 45, Part 1396.26). Involvement of the private sector in the provision of human services under POSC increased significantly following creation of the Title XX program. As late as 1973, 89% of all funding under Titles I, IV-A, X, XIV, and XVI of the Social Security Act being expended under POSC went to other public agencies. (See Table 2.1.). This is despite the fact that the overwhelming number of contracts were with the private sector (nonprofit and proprietary). By the end of the decade, however, the situation had clearly changed and the U.S. Department of Health and Human Services reported that approximately $1 billion out of the $2.5 billion in Title XX expenditures nationwide (40%) involved purchase of service contracts with the private sector (Mueller, 1980).

POSC IN THE 1980s

By the beginning of the 1980s, it could be safely said that POSC had become a major vehicle by which government provides human services. POSC for human services has become big business and is the preferred mode of human services delivery in many states. In 25 states, at least

TABLE 2.1
Purchase of Service Contracts by Type of Contractor

Contractor	Number of Contracts	Percentage of Contracts	Dollars (in millions)	Percentage of Dollars
Public	910	19.4	2,384	89.3
Nonprofit	3,337	71.2	262	9.8
Proprietary	438	9.3	21	.8
Total	4,485	100.0	2,669	100.0

SOURCE: Adapted from Wedel (1974, p. 58). Reprinted with permission.

50% of Title XX human services expenditures went for purchase of service contracts in fiscal year 1977, with some states expending substantially higher percentages (Mueller, 1978). In 12 other states, purchase of service contracts account for at least 40% of the Title XX human services activity, and virtually every state has at least some involvement with POSC.

THE FUTURE OF POSC

What does the future hold for POSC for human services? The answer appears to be continued reliance on POSC as the major mode of service delivery and the increasing involvement of private sector organizations—both nonprofit and proprietary—as contractors.

The American Public Welfare Association (APWA) foresees greater involvement of the private sector in POSC for human services in the near future due primarily to what it believes is the "philosophical bent" of the block grant approach (APWA, 1981). This view is shared by the International City Management Association (ICMA). The ICMA actively encourages its members to forge more public/private sector partnerships through the use of POSC and other approaches as a method of dealing with the diminishing resources for public sector programs (Rutter, 1981).

Recent research on state agency POSC activity under the Social Services Block Grant suggests that the overwhelming majority of SSBG POSC dollars are now going to private sector agencies (Martin, 1986). Table 2.2 compares fiscal year 1984 state Title XX POSC activity with fiscal year 1973 state Title XX POSC activity. As can be seen, although the distribution of contracts between public, nonprofit, and proprietary contractors has remained relatively stable, a dramatic shift in contracted dollars away from government contractors to nonprofit and proprietary contractors has taken place.

Proprietary contractors received less than 1% of the contracted dollars in 1973; they received almost 23% in 1984. The use of proprietary contractors appears to be tied directly to increased service activity in such areas as child day-care, residential treatment services, and home care services for the elderly and handicapped. In the future, POSC for human services will clearly have to deal with the presence of proprietary contractors and the competitive and market forces they inevitably will create.

What do all these changes and trends mean for the future of the human services industry? Will state and local governments continue their role in direct provision of services, or will POSC become the predominant or sole method of delivery? More important, what form of delivery is most efficient and effective in resolving individual, family, and community problems? These are the kinds of questions that must be addressed in the coming decade if human service systems are to be refined, improved, and strengthened. In the interest of addressing these questions in an orderly, systematic manner, we propose in the following sections a frame of reference for better understanding POSC and exploring its optimum utilization.

A FRAME OF REFERENCE FOR PURCHASE OF SERVICE CONTRACTING

If there was a clear-cut and definitive answer to questions on efficiency and effectiveness—that is, if we knew that either government, nonprofit, or proprietary agencies provided better quality service and achieved better results at a lower cost—there would be little need for further discussion on the subject. There are, however, no such clear and definitive answers on the subject. Across the 50 states practices on direct delivery and POSC vary greatly as to the type and volume of services contracted. This can make for a chaotic and unpredictable system within any given state. A study of POSC in one state concluded that, in the absence of standards for decision making in POSC, decisions tend to be controlled by power and political self-interest (Massachusetts Taxpayers Foundation, 1980). It is highly unlikely that such a system serves the best interests of the consumer or the public in terms of effectiveness, quality, relevance, or cost of services.

TABLE 2.2
Purchase of Service Contracting by
Fiscal Year and Type of Contractor

Contractor	Percentage of Contracts		Percentage of Dollars	
	FY-73	FY-84	FY-73	FY-84
Public	19.4	19.1	89.3	20.0
Nonprofit	71.2	66.9	9.8	57.1
Proprietary	9.3	14.0	.8	22.9
Total	100	100	100	100
	(N = 51)	(N = 36)	(N = 51)	(N = 36)

SOURCES: Wedel (1974, p. 59) and Martin (1986).

GUIDELINES FOR DECISION MAKING IN POSC

Perhaps because it is such a relatively young field of practice, the knowledge base about POSC is limited. Theoretical or conceptual underpinnings to POSC practices are rare. The purpose of this section is to establish a set of criteria as a frame of reference for addresssing the major questions about POSC in a rational and systematic way.

Two questions are explored: (1) For any given service, how can the best and most informed decisions be made about whether the service should be delivered directly by the government or purchased using POSC? and (2) If the decision is to use POSC, what approach will help to achieve the objectives for that particular program or service?

WHY STATES CONTRACTED FOR SERVICE—1970 to 1980

Before proposing a conceptual framework to understanding POSC as a field of practice, it is important to examine briefly some important empirical studies. Between 1970 and 1980, five studies were undertaken in an attempt to discover why POSC was growing so fast and becoming the preferred method of service delivery (Booz-Allen and Hamilton, 1971; Wedel, 1974; Benton, Field and Millar, 1978; Pacific Consultants, 1979; American Public Welfare Association, 1981). The following list summarizes reasons for using POSC cited by state social service agencies.

In the 1971 study, states cited these major reasons for using POSC:

- to provide for client choice and to satisfy unmet need
- to provide services not suitable to government delivery

- to increase the type and amount of service provided through the use of private (donated) funds
- to convert existing programs to new federal funding sources—the human services titles of the Social Security Act

In 1974, these were seen by states as the major benefits of POSC:

- The need to strengthen federal-state-private agency relationships
  - Increased federal and private funding
  - Increased public control and accountability
  - Increased cooperation between public and private sector
  - Strengthening the nonprofit sector
  - Desire to reduce the public payroll
- Increased consumer choice
  - Providing greater quantity, quality, and flexibility in choosing services
  - Providing new talent to clients of public social services
  - Availability of potential providers

The 1978 study divided its findings into major and lesser concerns affecting POSC decisions:

- Major Concerns
  - Tradition
  - Community politics and pressures
- Lesser Concerns
  - Availability of providers
  - Costs, matching funds

The 1979 study identified these four factors as influencing POSC decisions:

- Organizational structure of the government
- Nature of service to be provided
- Planning and budgeting considerations
- Philosophy

In the 1981 study states responded that these seven factors were responsible for increasing POSC activity:

- Public-private agency relationships
- Positive POSC experience in own or other states
- Federal encouragement of POSC
- Enhancement of client services
- Availability of contractors
- Cost savings
- Redirection of government agency away from direct service to management

IDENTIFYING COMMON THEMES

Distilling the findings of the foregoing studies yields some common themes or factors affecting decisions by states to purchase services. Falling into six main categories, fourteen factors emerge from this analysis. Each of these factors can be used to help determine the most appropriate delivery mix for each service or program.

PRODUCTIVITY, FISCAL AND COST CONSIDERATIONS

(1) Lowering the cost of services

- Is low cost an important, high priority consideration with this particular program?

(2) Increasing control over fiscal accountability

- Is fiscal accountability a high priority consideration?

(3) Increasing Service Outputs

- Is increasing service outputs a priority?
  Will either direct delivery or POSC accomplish this best?

PLANNING, DESIGNING, AND FUNDING CONSIDERATIONS

(4) Fit of service type to government or private agency delivery

- Is this a type of service particularly well suited to either public or private delivery? For example, is client advocacy involved? Must services be provided at night or on weekends?

(5) Flexibility in targeting resources to meet need

- Is it likely that funds may need to be moved quickly from one service to another as needs become more obvious?

(6) Availability and capability of contractors

- Is there an adequate number of capable contractors for this particular service?

(7) Utilizing multiple funding sources

- Are there advantages to cost sharing among a number of funding sources? Will it increase the dollars available?

IMPROVING SERVICE TO CLIENTS

(8) Improving the quality and outcomes of service

- Is quality of service or service outcomes a high priority consideration?

(9) Improving access to services

- Is increasing consumer choice or access important to the success of this program?

GOVERNMENTAL ORGANIZATIONAL AND
POLICY CONSIDERATIONS

(10) Government agency philosophy regarding POSC

- Has the governmental unit (state, county, city) taken a position favoring either POSC or government delivery?

(11) Capacity of government agency to deliver services

- Does the government agency have the necessary staff and other resources to provide services?

LEGAL REQUIREMENTS

(12) Legal requirements

- Are there laws that require or prohibit government delivery or POSC for this particular service?

POLITICS AND LOYALTIES

(13) History and tradition

- What have past POSC practices been with this particular service? What are the likely expectations for continuation of past POSC practices?

(14) Politics and political pressures

- Who supports government delivery and who supports POSC for this service? In what position are they to influence decisions about this particular program or service?

From this list, the relevant considerations for each program or service can be identified and analyzed, and a plan developed for POSC, direct delivery, or some combination of service provision. Table 2.3 illustrates how the fourteen factors can be used to work toward better informed decisions.

SELECTING AN APPROACH TO POSC

If a decision is made to use POSC, one additional issue needs to be considered: What approach should the government contracting agency use? Kettner and Martin (1985a) have defined two models of POSC: a partnership model and a market model.

The partnership approach to POSC is defined as "a set of policies and practices (on the part of the government contracting agency) which views government and the private sector as part of a comprehensive human services system, and where the determining factor in selection of contractors is a concern for the development and maintenance of the human services system" (Kettner & Martin, 1985a, p. 206). A government contracting agency following the partnership model would (1) emphasize the strengthening of working relationships between the government funding source and the service delivery agency, (2) be flexible and compromising in the development, negotiation, and administration of contracts, (3) make contracting decisions primarily on

TABLE 2.3

Guidelines for Decision Making in Purchase of Service Contracting (POSC)

Factors	Total Government Delivery Indicated	Mix of Government Delivery and POSC Indicated	Total POSC Indicated
Productivity, Fiscal and Cost Considerations			
(1) Lowering the cost of services is a high priority	No clear service delivery pattern indicated		
(2) Increasing fiscal control is a high priority	Yes	No	No
(3) Increasing service outputs is a high priority	No clear service delivery pattern indicated		
Planning, Designing, and Funding Considerations			
(4) Nature of service raises problems:			
• for government delivery	No	No	Yes
• for POSC	Yes	No	No
(5) Flexibility in targeting resources is a high priority	No	No	Yes
(6) Availability and capability of contractors:			
• there is an adequate number of capable contractors	No	Yes	Yes
• there are few capable contractors	No	Yes	No
• there are no capable contractors	Yes	No	No
(7) Funding considerations			
• a mix of public/private funding will increase resources	No	No	Yes
Improving Services to Clients			
(8) Improving quality and outcomes of service to clients is a high priority	No clear service delivery pattern indicated		
(9) Improving access is a high priority	No	Yes	Yes

TABLE 2.3 Continued

Factors	Total Government Delivery Indicated	Mix of Government Delivery and POSC Indicated	Total POSC Indicated
Government Organizational and Policy Considerations			
(10) Government agency philosophy promotes:			
• government delivery	Yes	No	No
• POSC	No	No	Yes
(11) Limited agency resources prohibit government delivery	No	No	Yes
Legal Requirements			
(12) Law requires:			
• government delivery	Yes	No	No
• POSC	No	No	No
Politics and Loyalties			
(13) History and tradition promote:			
• government delivery	Yes	No	No
• POSC	No	No	Yes
(14) Politics and pressures promote:			
• government delivery	Yes	No	No
• POSC	No	No	Yes

the basis of concern for the stability of the human services system, (4) be cautious about experimentation with differing modes of service provision, and (5) promote specialization, rather than competition, among contractors in order to capitalize on public/private sector strengths (Kettner & Martin, 1985a, p. 206).

In the partnership model of POSC, government and the private sector are viewed as partners in a joint-venture undertaking. The POSC process is viewed from the perspective of two equal partners attempting to maximize the human service system's outputs through joint action. Delivery options may include total contracting or a mix of government delivery and contracting. Where services are purchased, however, contracts will be developed and negotiated within the context of maintaining and strengthening the stability of the system. This approach involves a high degree of interaction between government agency staff and private agency staff around planning, designing, budgeting, monitoring, and evaluating.

The market model is defined as "a set of policies and practices (on the part of the government contracting agency) which encourages competition among potential contractors and, where like contractors are competing to provide a like service, price is the determining factor" (Kettner & Martin, 1985a, p. 206). The market model places a high value on cost efficiency. A government contracting agency following a market approach to POSC would: (1) emphasize development of criteria for measuring efficiency and effectiveness, (2) negotiate with a high degree of specificity on issues of performance expectations, program design, and budget, (3) make contracting decisions primarily on the basis of cost and price, other factors being equal, (4) encourage experimentation with alternative methods of delivering services, and (5) devote resources to the recruitment and development of a pool of potential contractors (Kettner & Martin, 1985a, pp. 206-207).

In the market model of POSC, the government contracting agency is seen as a buyer or purchaser of human services and the private sector contractor is seen as the supplier or seller. The contracting function is viewed as a procurement process with both sides attempting to maximize efficiency and effectiveness through precise definition of contract expectations. Generation of competition and the subsequent lowering of cost is an intended result of the market approach.

As Figure 2.1 illustrates, the partnership/market continuum suggests that contracting systems may not be "pure" types (i.e., either market or partnership), but possess aspects of both approaches in varying degrees.

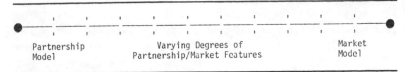

Figure 2.1: The partnership/market continuum.

The partnership/market continuum is also conceptualized as being dynamic in nature. Policies and administrative practices of the government contracting agency may move in either direction—toward partnership or market—depending upon the particular service under consideration and the nature of the agency's contracting objectives. Figure 2.2 illustrates a possible mix of contracting approaches within a particular government contracting agency.

Utilizing the partnership/market continuum as a frame of reference for planning and decision making can help answer some of the basic questions that underlie development of a sound POSC system. It encourages consideration of the reasons for contracting and directs decision makers toward certain activities and mechanisms, depending on the intent and expectations of the government contracting agency. The fourteen factors affecting decision making in POSC may once again be used to aid in selection of an appropriate approach for each program in the system. These factors and their effects on POSC decisions are depicted in Table 2.4.

Again, these factors are presented as a conceptual framework to be used to guide a POSC system toward achievement of its own objectives. In decision making about an approach to contracting, Factor 6— availability and capability of contractors—becomes critical. The market model is designed to promote competition for the purpose of procuring the highest prossible quality of service at the lowest possible cost. An adequate number of capable contractors is the sine qua non of competition. Where services are necessary and few contractors available, a partnership model must be adopted regardless of other factors.

Government organizational and policy considerations are of little help in deciding between a partnership or market approach. Much here will depend on the nature of the government agency's philosophy. A statement of philosophy might well include a preference for a partnership or market model, or indicate the circumstances under which either might be appropriate. Politics and loyalty considerations are most likely to favor a partnership model. Whether the influencing factor is history

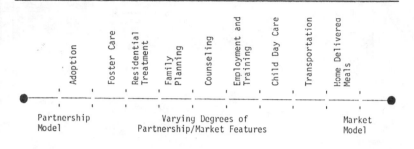

Figure 2.2: The illustration of where an agency's programs might fall on the partner-
ship/market continuum.

and tradition or political pressure, the issue is likely to be around
continued or increased funding for a specific set of programs or
providers. Under these circumstances, a market model is often an
unlikely alternative.

THE VALUE OF A
CONCEPTUAL FRAMEWORK FOR POSC

From an analysis of the early studies of factors affecting use of
POSC, it is evident that influencing factors have changed over time. At
one point funding considerations may emerge as predominant, at
another political pressures, and at still another service system considerations. In the absence of some framework for analysis, planners can
find decisions dictated by forces around them, with little predictability
and consistency in direction.

Utilizing the fourteen factors presented in this chapter as a framework for decision making can aid planners and administrators in
designing a more rational, consistent, and predictable system. The
factors can be used to develop an organizational philosophy around
provision of services and preferred options, which can provide an initial
sense of direction. Selected factors can be used to identify those services
for which either direct delivery or contracting is the only option. Where
either option is possible, the factors can be used to aid in selection of the
preferred option, depending on priorities in that particular situation.
They can be used to establish a rationale for decision making in
anticipation of political pressure rather than simply reacting or

TABLE 2.4

Guidelines for Decision Making in Selecting an Approach to Contracting

Factors	Partnership Approach Indicated	Market Approach Indicated
Fiscal and Cost Considerations		
(1) Lowering the cost of services is a high priority	No	Yes
(2) Increasing fiscal control is a high priority		
Planning, Designing, and Funding Considerations		
(3) Nature of service indicates:		
• collaboration between government and provider	Yes	No
• clear delineation and separation of roles and responsibilities	No	Yes
(4) Flexibility in targeting resources is a high priority	No	Yes
(5) Availability and capability of contractors:		
• there is an adequate number of capable contractors	No	Yes
• there are few capable contractors	Yes	No
• delivery capability needs to be promoted and increased	Yes	No
(6) Funding considerations		
• a mix of public/private funding will increase resources	Yes	No
Improving Services to Clients		
((7) Improving quality and outcomes of service to clients is a high priority	Either approach could be appropriate depending on Factor 5	
(8) Enhancing quality control is a high priority	Either approach could be appropriate depending on Factor 5	
(9) Increasing quantity and variety/improving access are high priorities	Either approach could be appropriate depending on Factor 5	
Government Organizational and Policy Considerations		
(10) Government agency philosophy promotes POSC	Yes	Yes
(11) Limited agency resources prohibit government delivery	Yes	Yes
(12) Law or policy requires government delivery	No	No
Politics and Loyalties		
(13) History and tradition promote collaboration	Yes	No
(14) Politics and political pressures promote POSC	Yes	No

acquiescing to pressures. And finally, they can be used to analyze programs and communitywide delivery systems and, in a planned way, to move them toward preferred options. Ultimately, use of influencing factors as a basis for analysis and decision making should lead to a more rational, planned approach to the critical questions associated with the issue of government delivery versus POSC.

SUMMARY

- POSC is both a new and an old concept. Purchase of service in various forms has been used by local governments since colonial times, but it was not until the 1960s that the federal government and the various states truly discovered the potential of the purchase of service contract.

- The changes in the human services titles of the Social Security Act created by the 1962 and 1967 Public Assistance Amendments and Title XX turned POSC for human services from a minor factor into the very significant component that it is today with substantial involvement on the part of the private sector.

- Trends indicate that POSC will continue to increase as a major funding and delivery vehicle in human services, at least for the forseeable future.

- Although POSC has increased dramatically over the past decade in human services, POSC systems developed by government agencies have often been inconsistent and unpredictable.

- Studies conducted between 1970 and 1980 indicate that there are some basic considerations that can be used as a framework for analysis in designing POSC systems.

- In designing POSC systems, two sets of decisions must be made for each program or service: (1) should the service be delivered directly by government or purchased from a community agency, and (2) if purchased, should the partnership model or market model be used?

- Using a framework for decision making can strengthen a POSC system by providing a rationale for current decisions and permitting a planned approach to achieve a preferred POSC system in the future.

Chapter 3

OVERVIEW OF THE POSC PROCESS

OBJECTIVES

By the end of this chapter the reader should be able to:

- Define the following key concepts:
    - Human services planning
    - Problem identification/problem analysis/needs assessment
    - Goals and objectives
    - Service need
    - Resource allocation
    - Direct provision
    - Steps in the POSC process

- Discuss or explain the following:
    - The logic of the planning process
    - Where POSC fits into the planning process
    - The steps in the POSC process

To many providers of human services, POSC seems like a closed system. Those who are in seem to stay in, and those who are not in do not seem to be able to get in. Some private agency directors may feel that they have a high quality service to offer but can't seem to get the state or the county to buy it.

All things being equal, providers should always have a fair chance to compete for available funds, although in practice this is not always the case. This chapter presents an overview of the human service planning and contracting process in the hope that both government contracting agencies and service providers, through a shared understanding of the process and its purposes, can work cooperatively to ensure that resources are used to provide the highest volume and best quality of services that available money can buy.

Delivering human services designed to solve community problems is a complex and involved process. A simple illustration might depict dollars earmarked for human services, on the one hand, and human problems and needs, on the other, as shown in Figure 3.1. Given the many human needs in every community and the limited resources available, how can we be certain that the dollars are spent in a way that ensures the best quality of service for the lowest possible cost? The answer is through some type of communitywide human services planning effort, a part of which involves POSC. This chapter will explore the broad context of planning for the meeting of human needs, and the place of POSC within that larger planning process.

THE PLANNING AND POSC PROCESS

Many volumes have been written about the planning process in human services and no attempt will be made here to duplicate those efforts. The purpose here is simply to put POSC into an appropriate context. The steps of the planning process are examined from the government contracting agency's perspective. They are purposely oversimplified for the sake of capturing a birds-eye view of a long and complex process. The process is depicted in Figure 3.2.

Communitywide human service planning is typically accomplished by a process in which community leaders solicit widespread input from all sectors of the community. Input, advice, and suggestions are then turned over to "planners," professionals who specialize in community-wide planning, for incorporation into the next fiscal year's human service plan. Ideally, problems and needs should be identified by those closest to them—people in need and those providing direct services to people in need. It often happens, however, that people with valuable insights into community needs keep silent throughout the planning process and wait to see what services will be funded. By that point many important decisions have already been made about priorities and

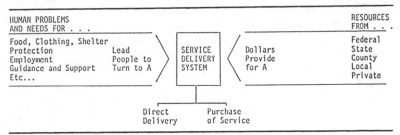

Figure 3.1: Planning turns dollars into services to meet needs.

resource allocation. Those with convictions about needs and services should become involved in the planning process early and remain involved throughout the complete cycle.

PROBLEM IDENTIFICATION/PROBLEM ANALYSIS/NEEDS ASSESSMENT

The purpose of this first step in the planning process is to establish a profile of community problems and needs. The product of this phase should be a numerical and statistical representation of needs and existing services, broken down by demographic characteristics (e.g., census tract, age, sex, ethnicity). Through the use of census data, employment data, rates of service, and other data, planners attempt to establish the number, location, and characteristics of people in need of each type of service. Typically a taxonomy or classification system will be used as a basis for defining a problem or need. An example of a taxonomy lists the following categories of problems or need for service:

An Example of a Human Services Taxonomy

The Number of People in _____ county who are having problems with the following:

Income

Gaining or maintaining employment

Learning or training

Personal/interpersonal adjustment

Health

Housing

Self-care

Nutrition

Abuse, neglect, exploitation

Child rearing and/or family

Alcohol and/or drug abuse

Safety and security

The analysis part of this first phase of the planning process attempts to go beyond a simple description of community problems and needs to an understanding of why they exist. Is family violence increasing, for example, because of increasing unemployment, because of increasing abuse of alcohol and drugs, because of inadequate skills to cope with stress, inadequate knowledge of alternative responses to marital and parenting stress, or some other cause? Problem analysis is not simply an academic exercise. It makes a difference in communitywide planning. Resources ultimately will be allocated to services that reflect a particular analysis or understanding of the reason for existence of a problem or need. It is important that community problems be carefully studied and weighed, and existing services not merely accepted as the only possible solutions. The insights of both providers and consumers at this point are critical to understanding causes and possible solutions.

Once needs are identified and analyzed, a systematic attempt to identify numbers of people in need is undertaken. This, together with an identification of available services, provides the basis for the annual establishment of goals and objectives.

USING GOALS AND OBJECTIVES TO ESTABLISH SERVICE PRIORITIES

Examining the profile of communitywide needs and services provides a beginning sense of direction for setting service priorities, usually stated as goals and objectives. These help to establish the parameters for the annual service plan. Utilizing problem identification, problem analysis, and needs assessment findings, planners and decision makers develop goals and objectives based on such factors as urgency of a particular need, needs of underserved special populations such as the elderly or minorities, the gap between needs and services, location of services in relation to need, or public support for a particular service. Providers and consumers should advocate for an open process that involves wide community participation in establishing service priorities.

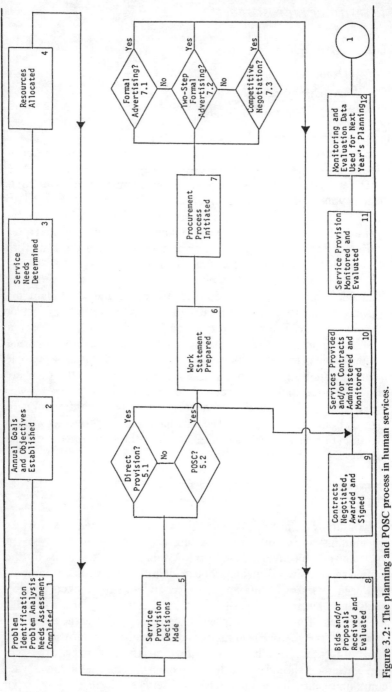

Figure 3.2: The planning and POSC process in human services.

DETERMINING VOLUME OF SERVICE NEED

Once goals and objectives are established, the volume of need for each type of service to be delivered in the upcoming program year is calculated. Taking into consideration such factors as size and location of populations in need, location and availability of existing services, and unmet need, a list of needed services is identified. Working from this list of services and using available data about service costs, resources needed to implement the plan are calculated.

RESOURCE ALLOCATION

Based on the estimated costs of service for the program year, a budget is submitted to a funding and decision-making body. Weighing this set of requests against all other requests for funding, and considering anticipated revenues, the decision-making body approves a budget for human services for the upcoming program year.

DIRECT PROVISION

Where services are to be provided directly by the government or other funding source, funds are channeled into programmatic areas and utilized for the direct provision of services to clients.

PURCHASE OF SERVICE CONTRACTING (POSC)

If it is decided that services can best be provided through the use of POSC, a series of steps is undertaken.

**Government Contracting Agency
Steps in the POSC Process**

- Work statement is prepared
- Procurement decisions are made and implemented
    - Formal Advertising
    - Two step Formal Advertising
    - Competitive Negotiation
- Bids and/or proposals are received and evaluated
- Contracts are negotiated, awarded and signed
- Service provision begins
- Contracts are administered and monitored

- Service provision is monitored and evaluated
- Data collected are used in subsequent planning cycles

These steps in the process form the basis of the remaining chapters of this book, and thus will be covered here only briefly for the sake of providing an overview. As we discuss each step, it will become clear that most of the content of the POSC process is covered from the government contracting agency's perspective. A word or two needs to be said about that at this point, and reinforced throughout the book.

It is clear from the flow chart in Figure 3.2 that the vast majority of functions and tasks in the POSC process are the responsibility of the government contracting agency. This, however, is not to say that these are within the exclusive domain of government contracting agency staff. The process, in a sense, "belongs" to the community and a process that is to be responsive to real problems and needs must involve contractors, consumers, and interested citizens. The government contracting agency, in response to the input provided, then carries out the will of the community.

Those who are interested in getting government contracts, we believe, can best accomplish that by understanding all appropriate roles and responsibilities, not simply their own. For the sake of presenting the counterpart to the government contracting agency steps in the POSC process, we suggest the following roles and responsibilities of the contractor:

Contractor's Role and Responsibilities in the POSC Process

- Remain actively involved in determining community needs and priorities throughout the planning year
- Provide government contracting agency with information that will help improve the efficiency and effectiveness of the POSC process
- Get copies of the Invitation for Bids (IFB) or Request for Proposals (RFP) when available
- Prepare and submit bids or proposals
- Provide service
- Provide data and information for monitoring and evaluation
- Provide information and feedback for the next planning cycle

---

Prospective contractor's input into the POSC process. When a contracting cycle begins, the relationship between a government contracting agency and prospective contractors changes in some significant ways. In most states laws restrict prospective contractor's involvement in the preparation of work statements or procurements to prevent even the appearance of favoritism in the awarding of contracts. Everything that happens must go "by the book." It is, however, not only acceptable but advisable that contractors and prospective contractors maintain a file of important observations or incidents to be compiled in an end-of-the-contract-year report to the government contracting agency. This type of feedback can be invaluable to those responsible for the POSC process in subsequent years. Special attention should be devoted to the quality of work statement. Too stringent and restricting a document can prohibit the flexibility sometimes required to meet complex human needs. Too vague a document can lead to poor quality and even fraudulent practices.

In addition, feedback on the impact of procurement practices, negotiation, monitoring, and evaluation can contribute to improvement of the process over time. The goal of a model system is that needs and concerns of consumers, contractors, and the government contracting agency all be considered and dealt with as effectively as possible throughout the process.

Work statement. Defining what is to be purchased is the function of the work statement. A complete work statement includes the following parts: (1) Service Definition, (2) Definition of Terms, (3) Enumeration of Standards, (4) Design Specifications, (5) Performance Specifications, (6) Definition of Units of Service, (7) Definition of Contract Objectives, and (8) Administrative and Reporting Requirements. These parts combine to describe, in as precise a language as possible, what the government contracting agency expects from the contractor. As will become evident in Chapter 4, specifying the details of service expectations in POSC is a task that requires a high level of knowledge, skill, and experience.

Procurement. The process by which a government contracting agency acquires goods and services is called "procurement." Many organizations, in fact, have procurement officers whose responsibility it is to handle all acquisitions. In POSC there are three major methods of procurement: formal advertising, two-step formal advertising, and competitive negotiation. When formal advertising is selected, the procurement mechanism used is called the "Invitation for Bids" (IFB).

When competitive negotiation is the choice, the mechanism is called the "Request for Proposals" (RFP). When two-step formal advertising is the process to be adopted, both the RFP and the IFB are used. These procurement processes are explained in detail in Chapter 5.

Bid and/or proposal evaluation. If an IFB is used as the procurement mechanism, responses will come in the form of bids. If an RFP is used, responses will be a proposal. Bids and proposals must be determined to be responsive and potential contractors to be responsible. Responsiveness means that a bid or proposal complies with all the provisions of the IFB or RFP. Contractor responsibility means that the potential contractor has the necessary skills, resources and reputation to carry out the requirements of the contract satisfactorily. When an IFB is used, the contract is awarded to the responsible bidder submitting the lowest responsive bid. When an RFP is used, criteria for evaluation of proposals will be specified in the RFP package. Once proposals are received by the government contracting agency, they are evaluated and scored, and a contract is awarded to the agency whose proposal scored highest according to preestablished criteria. Evaluation of bids and proposals also requires the skills of price and cost analysis, which are covered in Chapter 6.

Contract negotiation, award, and signing. Once a bid or proposal is evaluated favorably, if there are no unresolved differences between the government contracting agency and the contractor, a final contract can be drafted and signed. There may be instances, however, when the government contracting agency wishes to make an award, but has some questions or concerns about the bid or proposal. With a bid, there is no room for negotiation because all requirements have been predetermined and must be met as specified. If negotiations were to take place, losing bidders could challenge the procedures, claiming that the rules were changed. Bids must be accepted as submitted.

With proposals, however, there is room for negotiation. A government contracting agency may evaluate a proposal highly, yet may have concerns about selected parts. These concerns are itemized and submitted to a process of negotiation that, if successful, will result in revision of the proposal, contract award, and signing of a final contract document. Both government contracting agency and prospective contractor negotiators should be perfectly clear about contract objectives so that an opportunity to provide the best possible service results from the negotiations. The negotiation process is described in Chapter 7.

Contract administration. Once a contract is signed, a person is assigned to deal with the contractor on all questions, concerns, or activities that take place during completion of the contract. That person is called the "contract administrator." It is the contract administrator's role to represent the government contracting agency in dealings with the contractor, interpret the contract, monitor contract compliance, protect the rights of the government contracting agency, and process contract modifications. The details of contract administration are covered in Chapter 9.

THE VALUE OF HUMAN SERVICES PLANNING

Communitywide human services planning begins with the development of a profile of community social problems and needs. Resources are then allocated to fund services that will address identified needs. POSC has had a major impact on the service delivery systems in most communities. As methods of delivery are reevaluated, POSC is becoming the preferred option over direct government delivery for a wide range of services—from day-care for children to nursing care for the elderly. The quality of care provided for millions of clients in communities across the country can be influenced in many ways by the quality of the contract under which the care is provided. For this reason the knowledge and skills necessary for carrying out the requirements of POSC can have significance beyond the direct application to the POSC process. A soundly designed and well-administered POSC process can influence the effectiveness and efficiency with which a community or a state addresses its social problems and human needs.

SUMMARY

- POSC is part of a larger context or system of communitywide human services planning
- The communitywide planning process involves the following:
  - Identifying and analyzing community problems and assessing community needs
  - Setting communitywide goals and objectives
  - Designing the service delivery system
  - Allocating resources
  - Direct delivery of services or POSC
  - Monitoring
  - Evaluation

- POSC includes the following steps:
  - Preparation of the work statement
  - Procurement
  - Bid and/or proposal evaluation
  - Contract negotiation, award, and signing
  - Service delivery
  - Contract administration
  - Contract monitoring
  - Service evaluation
- Knowledge and skill in working with POSC systems can contribute to improved services.

Part II

DEVELOPING THE POSC CONTRACT

Chapter 4

THE WORK STATEMENT

OBJECTIVES

After completing this chapter, the reader should be able to:

- Define the following key concepts:
    - Work statement
    - Design specifications
    - Performance specifications
    - Inputs
    - Throughputs
    - Outputs
    - Outcomes
    - Service definition
    - Service tasks
    - Methodology
    - Standards
    - Units of service

- Discuss or explain the following:
    - The importance of writing effective work statements in POSC
    - The relationship between the systems model and the work statement
    - The elements of a work statement

- Perform the following function:
    - Given a case example, write a complete work statement

There is an important reason for beginning a discussion of the contracting process with the work statement. A work statement describes what the government contracting agency wants to buy, and developing the work statement forces the government contracting agency to think through that question clearly. At the onset it may sound simple. Everybody knows what is meant by day care, foster care or home delivered meals, don't they? Remember, however, that many tragedies have happened over the years in human services, some of which might have been prevented by more carefully written work statements.

What is a work statement? One definition is a description of the work and services to be performed and the methods that will be used (USDHEW, 1971). The work statement expresses what the contractor is to accomplish and determines whether the objectives sought will, in fact, be met (Buck et al., 1973). Drawing the best from existing definitions, we define a work statement as follows:

Definition of a Work Statement

The work statement is a document that expresses in clearly defined terms the expectations of the contract including the work to be performed and/or the results to be achieved.

The major challenge in writing good work statements is precision. The more precise, the better the work statement. The more ambiguous, the greater the potential for problems. Suppose, for the moment, that you are planning to purchase a car, and you decide to write up a set of requirements. Monthly payments must be under $300. Gas mileage must be 25 mpg or better. It should have air conditioning, AM/FM radio, power steering, two doors with hatchback, and the color should be red. You have a mental image of what you want to purchase. Yet someone could meet all of your requirements and the car may only remotely resemble what you had in mind. You may have envisioned a new car, whereas the seller can meet all the specifications with a used car. You may have envisioned a powerful sound system, whereas the seller can meet your requirements with the cheapest possible set of speakers. Your red may be a bright, brilliant color. The seller's may be almost orange.

Obviously all these differences in perception could be avoided through the use of more precise language. And yet, even when work statements are written on very simple items, precision is elusive. Recently a radio announcer commented in disbelief that Department of Defense specifications for purchase of a simple referee's whistle covered 16 pages! Imagine how much more difficult it is, then, to write a good work statement for the purchase of something as vague as a service that will help people solve their problems.

Suppose the service to be purchased is an educational service. How can you maximize the possibility that the teaching will be effective and that the students will learn? Suppose day care is to be purchased. How can you avoid "warehousing" and ensure a good quality of interaction between children and staff? These are the challenges that face the person who writes work statements for POSC.

PROSPECTIVE CONTRACTOR ASSESSMENT OF WORK STATEMENTS

Prospective contractors should be especially attentive to the ways in which the elements of work statements are defined. The work statement is the part of the contract that establishes the limits within which services will be provided. Requirements may focus on the types of clients to be served (e.g., low income, elderly, developmentally disabled). They may require a specialized type of intervention such as parent effectiveness training or psychological testing. Or the work statement could require that certain results be achieved such as reduction or elimination of reported incidents of child abuse among client families, a specified rate of job placement, or a percentage of clients that must remain drug free for one year. Whatever the requirements, it is critical that prospective contractors assess the work statement and their existing programs to determine the potential fit between contract expectations and ability to fulfill them.

THE CASE OF THE MISSED APPOINTMENTS

The State Department of Social Services was under heavy pressure about its Child Protective Services program. Over the past six months, stories of three deaths from abuse and neglect had hit the headlines in spite of the fact that the state legislature last year increased the number of CPS workers by 20%. It was clear that state staff alone could not keep up with this rapidly growing community problem. The help of many community agencies would have to be enlisted.

The decision of the state child welfare planners and policymakers was to utilize state staff to identify at-risk families, to have them do an assessment of family problems and needs, and to prescribe a mix of services that would be purchased from an array of existing private community agencies.

It was discovered three months into the program that only two-thirds of the expected number of families were receiving service from contractors. On investigation it was found that at-risk families were being identified, that assessments of problems and needs were being completed, that contracted services were being prescribed by case managers, but that families were not connecting with service providers. Service providers were telephoning the families or writing letters and setting up office appointments. The no-show rate was 33%, and the contracts allowed the contractors to bill for no-shows. The Department learned a difficult and expensive lesson that was corrected in the work statement the following year. Through the use of both design and performance specifications, they subsequently required outreach, in home appointments, and provided incentives for producing measurable changes in the family situation. The decline in the incidence of child abuse among at-risk families the following year was dramatic.

THE ELEMENTS OF A WORK STATEMENT

A complete and effective work statement need not be lengthy. It must, however, be clear and concise, avoiding the use of ambiguous and undefined terms. In order to understand how a work statement is constructed, it is necessary to understand its elements or component parts. We will, in this chapter, attempt first to identify, define, and describe the elements. Next we will explain how the elements fit together to define a service in a way that makes purchase of that service possible. Finally, we will present a format for writing a complete work statement. An example, following this format, can be found in Appendix A.

Elements to be discussed in this chapter essentially follow an outline format—that is, there are major headings, subcategories, and sub-subcategories. These elements are listed below.

The Elements of a Work Statement

- Design Specifications
  - Inputs
    - —Client characteristics
    - —Problem type and severity

—Staff characteristics
—Facilities and equipment
- Throughputs
  —Definition of service
  —Service tasks
  —Methodology
- Performance Specifications
  - Outputs
    —Definition of service completion
  - Outcomes
    —Definition of quality of life change for clients

To a prospective contractor, understanding a work statement is critical. Work statements are not typically laid out in an input-throughput-output-outcome format. However, in order to assess the fit of a program to contract expectations, it may well be worthwhile to analyze both work statement and program elements in these terms:

Element	Contract Expectations	Prospective Contractor's Analysis
Inputs		
Client characteristics	What clients are expected to be served under this contract? (age, location, ethnicity, etc.)	To what extent do our current clients match this profile?
Problem type and severity	What problem(s) and severity level(s) are expected to be addressed?	Do we now serve people with these problems and levels of severity, or is there reason to believe we could?
Staff characteristics	What types of staff will the contract require?	Do we now employ such staff or is there reason to believe we could hire them?
Facilities and Equipment	What facilities and/or equipment will be required?	Do ours meet the specifications or can they be modified, if needed?

Throughputs		
Definition of service	What type(s) of service(s) will the contract require?	Do we have experience with these types of services or would they be new services for us? (a new service may require more effort to establish credibility)
Service tasks	What tasks must be performed?	Do these tasks fit with our understanding of how this service should be delivered? If not, what adjustments need to be made?
Method of delivery	What method(s) of delivery are expected?	Do we have experience with these methods, or will they represent a change? Is there any reason to believe we cannot deliver this service as described?
Outputs		
Definition of a service completion	What will the contract require for a complete episode of service? Will payment be tied to outputs or completions?	Does this fit with our definition of a completion? What controls do we have over dropouts? Is there any reason to believe we could not meet output expectations?
Outcomes		
Definition of quality of life change	What outcomes are expected? What are the indicators? What	Do we have experience in measuring outcomes? Do we

| for clients | measurement tools will be used? Is payment tied to outcome? | have confidence in the measurement tools? Is there any reason to believe we could not achieve outcome expectations? |

Definitions and discussion of each of these elements of a work statement follows.

SPECIFICATIONS

The first concept necessary to the understanding and construction of work statements is a specification.

> **Definition of a Specification**
> A specification is a statement containing a detailed description or enumeration of particulars as to the expectations of the contract.

The work statement is made up of specifications, a listing of what must be performed and/or achieved to meet the terms of the contract. There are two kinds of specifications in POSC—design specifications and performance specifications.

Design specifications establish the framework or structure within which the service or activity will be carried out. They also define the details of process or procedure as well as workmanship, materials and goods, or dimensions and tolerances.

In home construction, for example, design specifications would establish the precise layout and square footage for each room, would require a particular type of lumber, and perhaps even state the ways in which various parts must be fastened together. The assumption is that if design specifications are followed to the letter, the results will be what the purchaser intended—a home of adequate size, stability, durability, and attractiveness to meet expectations and make it worth the price.

In human services, design specifications focus on those elements that make up the service provision system. In a child abuse prevention program, for example, design specifications would include provision of family counseling services, crisis shelter, day care, parent aid, transportation, and other relevant services. For each service a detailed description of acceptable methods and standards would be provided. As with home construction, the assumption is made that if design specifications are followed conscientiously, the result will be what both parties to the contract want—a family able to provide a loving and nurturing environment for its members and capable of coping with the day-to-day stresses it faces.

Peformance specifications differ significantly from design specifications. Instead of focusing on the structure, materials, process, or workmanship, they focus on what is expected as a result of service. Performance specifications are statements that establish criteria by which the end products or results of service can be evaluated. In a way, performance specifications are a way of stating, "Here are the results we expect. How you achieve the results is up to you." Returning to the home construction example, the buyer would focus on home "performance." The house would have to withstand the elements such as heat, wind, and rain without leaking, cracking, or falling apart. The electricity and plumbing would be expected to work without breakdown. The room sizes would be expected to be adequate to accommodate the purposes for which they were intended.

In human services, performance specifications focus on completions and/or results. In a child abuse prevention project, the contract might specify that at least 75% of the families referred for Parent Effectiveness Training must complete the course. This leaves design (classroom content, teaching methodology) up to the contractor and simply specifies that a minimum number of completions must be achieved. If the contract objective is that families should put effective parenting techniques into practice, then performance specifications would require that no less than a specified percentage of families who complete the Parent Effectiveness Training course successfully demonstrate the use of at least 6 techniques in the role-playing situation between parents and children. Again, if this is the only specification, design is left to the provider.

Design and performance specifications are not mutually exclusive. It is possible and even common to have both in a work statement. The only stipulation is that there must be a good fit between them. Design specifications must not be so stringent and restrictive that they create barriers to compliance with performance specifications. In selecting an approach to POSC, design specifications are more likely to be used in a partnership model; performance specifications are more likely to be used in a market model. More will be said about this later in this chapter.

INPUTS, THROUGHPUTS, OUTPUTS, AND OUTCOMES

In order to understand how to develop the parts of a work statement, it is important first to know how a human service program is structured and designed. The model to be used for analysis of program design is the systems model. Using this model, components that make up the system can be categorized as inputs, throughputs, outputs, and outcomes. Inputs are raw materials and resources. Throughputs are the change or conversion processes. Outputs are the products and outcomes are results.

In a product-producing organization—an appliance manufacturing plant, for example—the components or parts of the system might be categorized as follows:

Systems Components of an Appliance Manufacturing Plant		
Component	Definition	Example
Inputs	Raw materials and resources	Metal, rubber, plastic, wiring, etc. Plant, machinery, employees, etc.
Throughputs	Processing systems	Converting raw materials to parts; converting parts to appliances
Outputs	Products	Completed appliances produced (e.g., toasters, blenders, etc.)
Outcomes	Results	Customer satisfaction with product and performance

In human services, the elements of program design include the following:

Systems Components of a Family Counseling Agency		
Component	Definition	Example
Inputs	Raw materials and resources	Clients, staff, facilities, equipment
Throughputs	Processing systems	The helping process (e.g., counseling, parent training, etc.)

| Outputs | Products | Serviced clients—those who have completed the service process |
| Outcomes | Results | Improved family functioning |

Defining each of these components for the service to be provided forms the basis for a precise and effective work statement.

INPUTS

In defining inputs, a range of characteristics may be specified about the clients who are to be served by this program. First, the client population itself must be defined. This is usually done in terms of geographical boundaries, age, income, or other descriptive factors. In defining the client population, it may be necessary to specify a problem type (e.g., employment, housing, family violence) and level of severity. If clients must meet certain eligibility criteria to receive services, these criteria should be identified and written out in the draft stages of developing the work statement.

Second, if requirements relative to space, location, equipment, personnel, or other resources are to be imposed, these definitions should also be written out for later use. An illustration of how this might be done for a transportation service follows:

Sample Worksheet for Developing a Definition of Terms Section for a Work Statement	
Inputs	*Specifications*
Clients	People who are isolated from needed services due to lack of transportation
Eligibility factors	Residents of Bradford County 65 years old or older; Annual income of $10,000 or less; Unable to access public transportation due to handicap or distance
Staff	Over 21; Able to drive a vehicle; Possesses a valid chauffeur's license
Vehicles	Must accommodate wheelchairs

THROUGHPUTS

The processing system for services consists of the services offered, and can be broken down into three elements: definition of service, service tasks, and method of delivery.

Throughput Work Statements Elements

- Service Definition
- Service Tasks
- Method of delivery

Developing a service definition requires that precise, concrete, and measurable limits be established for the scope of services. The purpose is to ensure that contractors understand the nature of the service to be delivered. This is a point where a service taxonomy or classification system can be useful. The United Way of America has developed the United Way of America Service Identification System (UWASIS) to aid in defining services. Over 231 services are labeled and defined. Communication is greatly facilitated when common definitions are used. An example from the UWASIS directory is prejob guidance, defined as follows:

> Pre-Job Guidance is a program designed to help individuals who need to learn the basic tools of obtaining employment to suit their particular skills and talents. (United Way of America, 1976, p. 8)

Service definitions can be very brief. The length will depend on the complexity of the service. The purpose of the service definition is to narrow the focus of the service being purchased, and to separate it from other types of services.

The second throughput element is service tasks. Service tasks define all of the activities to be included within the scope of the service definition. Service tasks are important in POSC because they help to narrow down and define what will be paid for in the contract. UWASIS, for example, includes the following activities within the definition of prejob guidance (United Way of America, 1976, p. 8):

Sample Service Tasks for Prejob Guidance

- Vita or resumé preparation
- Dress and personal appearance

- Filling out applications
- Writing letters applying for a job
- Respond to a job ad
- Interview techniques
- Taking employment tests
- Providing general orientation to occupational choices

Listing service tasks serves a useful function. Such activities as counseling for personal problems, transportation, or day-care services would not be covered under a contract for prejob guidance and would not be reimbursed if performed. Only those service tasks specified as fitting within the context of the service definition are considered acceptable and reimburseable. The listing of service tasks, therefore, becomes a mechanism for limiting the scope of service and should be analyzed carefully by prospective contractors.

The third throughput element is method of delivery. Specification of methods requires a definition of how the service is to be provided. Provision of meals, for example, can be accomplished in a congregate meal program or literally delivered to the door. Counseling methods can include individual, family, or group. Training methods can include classroom, tutorial, or self-study. UWASIS, for example, defines the methods for prejob training as follows: "The program may operate on a one-to-one or on a group basis" (United Way of America, 1976, p. 8). Development of service definition, service tasks, and method of delivery completes the throughput elements.

OUTPUTS

Once the processing system has been conceptualized and defined, the next component to be addressed is that of outputs. In human service terms, outputs are service completions. In production terms, outputs would be the complete products that come off the assembly line, such as automobiles, vacuum cleaners, or paper cups. The purpose of the throughput or processing system is to turn inputs (raw materials) into outputs (finished products). In human services a processing system or service (throughput) is designed to turn inputs (clients with problems) into outputs (clients who complete a service process) in the hope that this will improve the client's quality of life (outcome). It is not unusual in human services for outputs to be left undefined. Frequently program descriptions focus on the plan for service provision (such as counseling, meals, foster care) without defining a service completion. The assumption, apparently, is that services will be provided indefinitely, until no longer needed.

In POSC, however, there are clearly some advantages to defining the outer limits of an episode of service (and clearly some problems when this is not done). Perhaps the simplest illustration of these advantages is with job training. If it takes eight training sessions to teach a person the skill of welding, then it is important to know whether a trainee attended one, two, or all eight training sessions. Should a contractor, for example, be held accountable for a trainee getting and holding a job if the trainee drops out of training after two sessions? Is a contractor paid for dropouts? Whose responsibility is it to keep clients in service as long as possible? If no attempt is made to define output, these questions may never be addressed.

The same concept holds true also for family counseling, homemaker services, or other services. They tend to be designed so that if clients receive the full complement of services, they will realize an improvement in their situation (such as better interpersonal relationships or improved home management skills). When output is clearly defined, those who complete the service process are distinguished from those who do not. Even if those who fail to complete the service process fare as well as or better than those who do, the information is still important for monitoring, evaluation, and future program planning purposes.

OUTCOME

The final element to be addressed in conceptualizing program design is that of outcome.

Definition of Outcome

An outcome of service is defined as a change in the quality of life of the person or persons who received the service.

The concept of outcome or results cuts to the heart of the reason for existence of every human service program. Programs are funded not because they promise to "provide" something, but rather because they promise to have an impact on a community social problem such as unemployment, crime, or child abuse. Ultimately, then, the measure of success is whether or not the impact was achieved.

Outcomes are often elusive and difficult to define in observable and measurable terms. What, for example, is the expected outcome of family

counseling? Presumably to improve the quality of interpersonal relationships of family members. Such a definition may be acceptable to a
therapist, supervisor, or agency administrator, but to a contract
monitor or evaluator it presents problems. How will the contract
monitor know whether interpersonal relationships have been improved?

For some services (such as job training) precise definition of outcome
is not difficult (e.g., placement in a job beginning at least at minimum
wage for at least one year). For others, some type of pre- and
postassessment often must be included in the program design—that is,
calculating a problem profile on a series of scales before and after
treatment and using the difference as a measure of outcome.

Sometimes it becomes necessary to separate outcomes into two
types—intermediate and ultimate. Some programs, such as residential
treatment, may offer a range of services (e.g., one-to-one counseling,
special education, and recreation therapy). For each service, there is an
expected outcome. For counseling, it may be to improve self-esteem; for
education, increased knowledge and skill; for recreation, development
of healthy outlets for stress. Each of these, however, would be classified
as an intermediate outcome. Ultimately, the test of successful residential
treatment is adjustment to living outside the institution, and a measure
of quality of adjustment would be considered the ultimate outcome.
Typically the breakdown into intermediate and ultimate outcomes is
necessary only when a mix of services is designed to produce an overall
improvement in the quality of life.

SPECIFYING QUALITY AND QUANTITY

Before the work statement is ready for preparation, two additional
factors must be addressed: the issues of quality and quantity.

**The Meaning of Quality and Quantity
In the Work Statement**

QUALITY = STANDARDS
QUANTITY = UNITS OF SERVICE

Quality refers to the establishment of a minimum level of acceptability
of design or performance, and is accomplished by the setting of
standards. Quantity refers to the establishment of a measure of volume,
and is accomplished by defining units of service.

STANDARDS

A standard is defined as follows:

Definition of a Standard

A specification accepted by recognized authorities that is regularly and widely used and that has a recognized and permanent status. (Buck et al., 1973)

Standards protect the consumer and ensure a minimum level of quality in the product or service. No one wants to pay for food that is spoiled, cars that will not start, or home repairs that fall apart. We are protected in many of the products and services we purchase every day by standards. Health departments inspect restaurants using a set of health and hygiene standards. Cities inspect construction work using established building code standards.

Standards, in human services, can apply to inputs, throughputs, outputs, or outcomes as defined in the foregoing sections of this chapter, and as illustrated in the following examples.

Examples of Standards

System Component	Element	Example
Input	Client eligibility	Clients must be first offenders who have been reported for committing an offense that fits the definition of minor abuse and/or neglect.
	Staff	Counseling services must be performed by a person with a masters degree in social work or psychology from an accredited program.
	Facilities	Child-care facilities must provide a minimum of 150 square feet per child and meet all health and hygiene standards established by the County Health Department.
Throughput	Service	Child care includes supervision of children between the hours of 6:00 a.m. and 6:00 p.m. at least 5 days per week and must in-

		clude a planned program of activities drawn from the county's approved list of activities that covers all hours of operation.
	Service tasks	An assessment of each child's social and emotional needs will be completed by the end of the first week of service.
	Method of delivery	A maximum of ten parent training sessions may be provided in groups. Maximum size of groups shall be 12.
Output	Completion	Trainees must complete at least eight sessions that must include the first and the last sessions to complete the program.
Outcome	Quality of life factor	Client families must be free of any reported incident of child abuse and/or neglect for a period of two years.

UNITS OF SERVICE

Measures of volume in commercial production tend to follow standard definitions such as gallons, pounds, or yards. These measures are critical to the calculation of volume of production, distribution, and sale as well as in calculation of costs. In response to the question, "How much gasoline did we pump today?" a station owner does not want to hear "a lot" or "not much." He wants a precise answer in terms of gallons. By the same token in the delivery of human service programs, one must be able to calculate volume of delivery for a day, a week, a month, or a year. These are calculated by defining units of service.

There are five types of units of service:

Five Types of Units of Service

(1) A time unit, such as an hour of counseling or a day of day care.
(2) An episode unit, such as counseling session or a referral.
(3) A material unit, such as a food basket or article of clothing.
(4) An output unit, such as graduation from a training program.
(5) An outcome unit, such as being drug free for one year.

The time, episode, and material units are options that can be utilized to measure the volume of throughput or process. The output unit measures output, and the outcome unit measures volume of outcome. More than one type of unit of service may be used in a single contract.

Putting all of these work statement elements together in a systems framework yields the graphic illustration depicted in Table 4.1. It should be noted that the examples used are only abbreviated statements shortened for the sake of displaying them in chart form. In an actual work statement each word would be examined to determine if more than one interpretation might be drawn from the use of that term. If more than one interpretation is possible, the term will need to be defined. Terms such as "minor abuse" and "minor neglect" would fall into this category.

WRITING THE WORK STATEMENT

Once each of the foregoing elements has been defined to the satisfaction of those drafting the statement, some decisions must be made about the use of specifications. The decisions involve a selection of design specifications (inputs and throughputs) and/or performance specifications (outputs and outcomes). Either or both may be used. The major consideration, if both are used, is that they be compatible. Design specifications should not be so stringent that they prevent achievement of performance specifications. An important consideration in selecting between design and performance specifications is a decision about whether the market model, the partnership model, or some combination is to be used.

PARTNERSHIP/MARKET CONSIDERATIONS

As defined in Chapter 2, the partnership model attempts to support and promote the stability of the human services system whereas the market model attempts to promote competition in the interest of driving down the cost of services. In addition to those decision criteria identified in Chapter 2, there are some important issues to consider in selecting an approach.

First is the issue of cost and use of resources. Selecting a partnership model for a service where competition (and use of a market model) is possible may mean that resources invested are not serving as many clients as they would through the market model. On the other hand,

TABLE 4.1
The Elements of a Work Statement Depicted within a Systems Framework

	Design Specifications Include Inputs and Throughputs		Performance Specifications Include Outputs and Outcomes	
	Inputs	Throughputs	Outputs	Outcomes
Definition	Raw materials and resources	Service provision or conversion process	Service products discharged from the system	Quality of life change for clients as a result of service
Elements	Definition of client population Eligibility criteria Definition of problem type to be served Measurement of problem severity Definition of requirements for Staff Space Location Equipment, etc.	Definition of service Service tasks Methodology	Definition of service completion	Definition of intermediate outcome Measurable change in problem severity as a direct result of service provided Definition of ultimate outcome Measurable change as a long-term result in terms of social adjustment and coping skills

Examples

Families at risk of abusing children, with documented complaints of minor abuse and/or neglect and who volunteer for treatment

Residents of Jackson County

Families who are determined to be under moderate to severe stress as measured by the Family Stress Scale

Counseling staff must possess MSW degrees

Child abuse and neglect prevention counseling is defined as an interpersonal interaction between counselor and client designed to determine sources of stress and develop methods to alleviate it

Service tasks

Collect background data (social history) on family

Administer Family Stress Scale

Develop and analyze stress profile

Discuss profile with family

Develop a plan

Etc.

Methodology—Either one-to-one, family, or group counseling may be used

Completing the counseling schedule as proposed in the case plan shall be defined as a service completion

Intermediate outcome

Reduced stress as measured on the Family Stress Scale

Ultimate outcome

No incidents of abuse or neglect in long-term follow-up

Positive use of skills to cope with stress

Standards May Be Established for Inputs, Throughputs, Outputs, and/or Outcomes

Units of Service May Be Defined in Terms of Throughputs, Outputs, and/or Outcomes driving down costs in the interest of serving more clients means little if the quality and effectiveness of the service suffers in the process. The optimum approach is the one that will yield the best possible results for the lowest cost.

In selecting an approach to POSC, results must always be weighed equally with cost. Costs can be lowered for any service if no attention is paid to considerations of quality and results. Government contracting agencies, however, are responsible for all of these factors—cost, quality, and results—and cannot simply choose one to the exclusion of the others. Close working relationships with clients and direct service providers can be helpful in selecting the optimum partnership-market mix designed to get the best possible service to the greatest number of clients.

The significance of this decision for POSC is that attempts to drive down the cost (market model) can only be undertaken if there are some assurances (i.e., some measurable indicators) that costs are not reduced at the expense of destroying the program's effectiveness. To give a simple example, if it costs $1000 a week to run a day-care service for 10 children (a unit cost of $100 per child per week), unit costs could be cut in half by simply accepting 20 children while making no adjustments in staff, space, food, equipment, or other necessary resources. Clearly, in using such an approach the quality of the service may be adversely affected and renders this method unacceptable even though more children are served at a lower cost.

The implications for the partnership/market models are that, unless performance specifications (outputs and outcomes) are used, the market model cannot be responsibly adopted. In the absence of clear measures of output and outcome, the approach selected must necessarily be toward the partnership end of the continuum. In short, the partnership/market decision will be influenced by the type of data to be collected, as indicated in Figure 4.1.

The assumption is, of course, that data collected will be used for monitoring and evaluation purposes, and that the contract will allow for adjustments if it appears that the quality and/or results of service are deteriorating.

STEPS IN WRITING A POSC WORK STATEMENT

The foregoing sections of this chapter are intended to establish an understanding of the basic terms, concepts, principles, and issues related

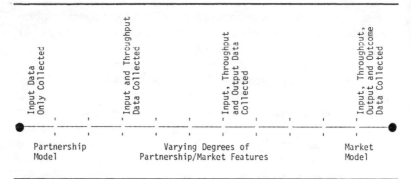

Figure 4.1: Relationship between data collected and the partnership/market continuum.

to the development of a work statement. In this section this knowledge will be applied to a systematic, step-by-step process designed to produce a complete work statement. Although the concepts, taken one at a time, may seem rather simple, the reader should be warned that writing effective work statements is hard work and that skill comes with practice.

This step-by-step process is intended to follow a logical thought process from the first point of problem identification through writing a complete work statement. Completion of the first eleven steps should provide all the materials necessary to compile the work statement. The final step is to put it all into an order that is logical for the prospective contractor. It is also important that prospective contractors understand the techniques of work statement development so that, where improvements are needed, suggestions can be offered with a full knowledge of what is required.

Step 1: Identify the problem to be solved. What is the problem? Whose expectations must be met for the problem resolution to be considered satisfactory?

Step 2: Identify the population to be served. Who has the problem? What limitations are placed on participants by eligibility factors? What assessment instruments, if any, will be necessary to determine problem type or severity? Write out all requirements or limitations relative to the population to be served.

Step 3: Develop the service definition. Write out a specific, operational definition of the service.

Step 4: Identify the tasks to be included. What tasks or activities will be paid for? What will not? What are the applicable standards? What are the applicable units of service? Write them out.

Step 5: Identity the acceptable methodologies. Should any limitations be placed on the ways in which the service tasks can be carried out? Write them out.

Step 6: Establish criteria for staffing, facilities, equipment, resources. What criteria should be established for the types of personnel who will carry out the tasks identified in Step 4, using the methodologies identified in Step 5? Are there applicable standards? What criteria should be established for facilities, equipment, or other resources? Write them out.

Step 7: Define a service completion. What constitutes a completion of one episode of service? Define what will be paid for and what will not. Are there applicable standards and units? Write them out.

Step 8: Define outcome or result. What results are expected? Define what will be paid for and what will not. Are their applicable standards and units? Write them out.

Step 9: Identify terms that need to be defined. Go through all sections and pick out terms that are potentially ambiguous. Give them specific, operational definitions. Write them out.

Step 10: Develop the contract objectives. What volume of each type of service or performance will be purchased? Write out the objectives.

Step 11: List data collection, recording, and reporting requirements. What kinds of reports will be required? What are the implications of these reports for data collection? Are specific forms required for either data collection or reporting? Write out all requirements.

Step 12: Put the work statement in order.

Proposed Format for a POSC Work Statement

I.	Service Definition
II.	Definition of Terms
III.	Enumeration of Standards
IV.	Design Specifications
	Input Elements
	Service Tasks
	Methodology
V.	Performance Specifications
	Output Definitions
	Outcome Definitions

VI.   Units of Service
VII.   Contract Objectives
VIII. Administrative and Reporting Requirements

WORK STATEMENT DEVELOPMENT EXERCISE

Saguaro County has determined that many of its senior center's programs have become limited essentially to noon meals and that the goals of active recreation and socialization programs have not been met in most cases. A decision has been made to attempt to correct these deficits by developing a more thorough and precise work statment for the next fiscal year.

Specifically, the following problems have been identified:

- Most centers revolve around the noon meal program. People arrive around 11:30 a.m. and are gone by 1:00 p.m.
- Center managers say that they have no control over the situation—that people just come to "eat and run."
- Many meal program participants state that they do not wish to become involved in activities because center managers run things their own way and are not interested in input from seniors.

In general, there is a feeling on the part of county officials that the programs have deteriorated, both in the quality and the level of activity. County supervisors are getting many complaints about the poor quality of programs, and the supervisors have indicated to the Director of Human Services that they would like the programs improved and the problems addressed.

Assume that a separate work statement has been written for meals and that this work statement is being designed strictly for the provision of additional recreation and socialization activities. The intent is to develop an active program with regular recreation and socialization activities before and after meals with participation by a majority of those who come for meals.

I. In preparation for developing a work statement, write out the following definitions:

- Inputs
  - Client definition
  - Staff definition for staff who will work in the recreation and socialization program

- • Facilities and equipment
- Throughputs
  - • Service definitions for recreation and socialization (these may be defined separately as two different services if you prefer)
  - • Service tasks
  - • Methodology
- Output
- Outcomes
- Standards
- Units of Service
- Volume of Service to be Purchased
- Reporting Requirements

II. Write out each section as indicated in Steps 1 through 11 presented in this chapter.

III. Organize these definitions into a work statement, using the following format:

I.	Service Definition
II.	Definition of Terms
III.	Enumeration of Standards
IV.	Design Specifications
V.	Performance Specifications
VI.	Unit of Service Definitions
VII.	Contract Objectives
VIII.	Administrative and Reporting Requirements

Chapter 5

PROCUREMENT

OBJECTIVES

By the end of this chapter the reader should be able to:

- Define the following key concepts:
  - Procurement
  - Formal advertising
  - Competitive negotiation
  - Two-step formal advertising
  - Responsiveness
  - Responsibility
  - Invitation For Bids (IFB)
  - Request for Proposals (RFP)
  - Sole source

- Discuss or explain the following:
  - The appropriate uses of formal advertising, competitive negotiation, and two-step formal advertising
  - The application of sole source procurement to POSC for human services

- Perform the following functions:
  - Analyze differing human services POSC situations and select the most appropriate procurement
  - Identify the major steps in formal advertising and competitive negotiation
  - Specify the component parts of a request for proposals (RFP) package

---

To procure means simply "to purchase" or "to buy." You "procure" something every time you go to the grocery story. Procurement also refers to the process by which government agencies acquire supplies, equipment, and services, including human services. There are several different types of procurement, and it is important that both government contracting agency and prospective contractor understand which procurement is being utilized. In this chapter, three competitive procurements (formal advertising, competitive negotiation, and two-step formal advertising) and one noncompetitive procurement (sole-source) are covered. The two basic documents (the invitation for bids and the request for proposals) most frequently used in procurements are also presented.

Why must procurement be so complicated? Why not simply send government employees out shopping? To answer that question, simply pick up a newspaper and you're likely to find a story about problems in government purchasing—overcharges, waste, fraud, and many other problems. In order to get the best buy and to be sure everyone has a fair chance to sell their products or services to the government, it is necessary to go through formal procurement procedures.

When a decision is made to utilize a particular competitive procurement, the decision also dictates the type of procurement document that will be used. The relationship between each of the three competitive procurement processes and the two basic procurement documents is illustrated in Figure 5.1. Formal advertising uses the invitation for bids (IFB) and competitive negotiation uses the request for proposals (RFP). Two-step formal advertising is a combination of competitive negotiation and formal advertising and uses both the request for proposals and the invitation for bids.

FORMAL ADVERTISING

Formal advertising, also known by such names as "bidding," "sealed bidding," and "competitive bidding," is the procurement preferred by the federal government and most state and local governments (Council of State Governments, 1975). This preference for formal advertising comes from its long history of satisfactory use in the procurement of supplies and equipment and from the general belief that formal advertising is the most open and competitive of all procurement processes. Formal advertising can be defined as follows:

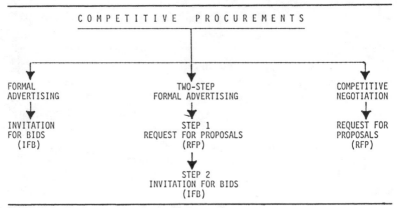

Figure 5.1: The relationship between procurement types and procurement documents.

Definition of Formal Advertising

The means of selecting a contractor through the use of a competitive procedure that includes solicitation of bids and the awarding of contracts to the responsible bidder submitting the lowest responsive bid. (General Services Administration, n.d.)

In order to utilize formal advertising effectively in POSC for human services, three conditions must be satisfied by the procurement:

- The contracting agency must know exactly what it wants to purchase and must have developed a work statement.
- The contracting agency must be willing to make price the major decision criterion in contract award.
- Competition must be anticipated in the procurement to ensure that market forces can be used to establish a fair service price.

Under formal advertising, the contracting agency is not seeking to negotiate service specifications or contractual terms with potential contractors; its only interest is in securing firm bids, or offers, for the delivery of the service.

Formal advertising has not been widely used in POSC for human services because contracting agencies have had difficulty in satisfying the foregoing three conditions for its use. In human services there is often a need to consider such nonprice factors as the service delivery history and staff qualifications of prospective contractors. Often, too, there is no competition for many human services. These factors have caused most state and local government contracting agencies to exclude formal advertising from their POSC activities.

Recently, a number of state and local government contracting agencies have begun using formal advertising for some selected human services. Over half of all Title XX state agencies today report some use of formal advertising in POSC for human services (Martin, 1986). Child day-care and homemaker services are two human services that are frequently procured using formal advertising.

THE CASE OF THE LATE BID

Health Services for the Elderly is a private, nonprofit home health agency that provides in-home services to elderly people who are homebound. Through word-of-mouth publicity, they were overwhelmed with requests for service, but fewer than half of their clients were able to pay. As a new agency, they found their resources stretched to the limit. Then came an opportunity to cover the costs of serving indigent clients. An Invitation for Bids was put out by the state to provide precisely the types of services they had been providing. The money earned from this contract would allow them to add staff and provide better quality services to their indigent clients. The director asked the nurse and the social worker to get the IFB, study it, and prepare the bid. They had great difficulty finding adequate time to get together. Time was running out. Finally they prepared the bid and turned it in for typing, with two hours to go until the deadline.

In the middle of typing the cover letter to accompany the bid, the electric typewriter quit. By the time the problem had been fixed and the letter typed, only 25 minutes remained until the announced closing time (12 noon) for bid submissions. The agency was located three miles from the government contracting agency's headquarters. The director was still confident that the bid could be submitted on time.

On the way, the director encountered a massive traffic jam, and arrived with the bid ten minutes late. Under the procedures outlined in the invitation for bids, the government contracting agency was unable to accept the late bid. As it turned out, Health Service for the Elderly submitted the lowest bid and would have received the contract. The agency lost a major POSC contract and the government wound up paying more for the service than it otherwise might have.

THE FORMAL ADVERTISING PROCESS

Formal advertising places a high degree of responsibility on prospective contractors to maintain a continuous awareness of expectations at each point in the process. They are expected to secure bid packages, attend the bidder's conference, and calculate and submit an exact bid within the time frame specified. There is little room for flexibility in the process.

As the name suggests, formal advertising is a highly structured procurement, and includes eight major steps:

Steps in Formal Advertising

Step 1: IFB package prepared.
Step 2: Procurement announced.
Step 3: IFB packages distributed.
Step 4: Bidder's conference held.
Step 5: Submission, opening, and recording of bids.
Step 6: Bids determined responsive.
Step 7: Contractor determined responsible.
Step 8: Contract awarded.

STEP 1: IFB PACKAGE PREPARED

The initial step in utilizing formal advertising is the development of the IFB package by the government contracting agency. The IFB package, at a minimum, always contains a work statement, contractual terms and conditions, and a section for prospective contractors (or bidders) to enter the amount of their bid and sign the document. Because of its construction, an IFB package can serve three purposes: (1) the invitation to bid that is sent to prospective contractors, (2) the bid itself that is returned by the prospective contractor, and (3) the resulting contract.

Three Purposes Served by an IFB Package

- the invitation for bids.
- the bid itself.
- the contract.

At the top of the state of Arizona's IFB cover page the words *BID OFFER AND CONTRACT* are highlighted in bold print. These words serve to warn prospective contractors that when they complete, sign, and submit a bid, an offer in the legal sense of the term comes into existence. If a bid is accepted by the state of Arizona, a contract can automatically come into being because the IFB package also meets all the necessary tests of contract formation.

STEP 2: PROCUREMENT ANNOUNCED

When a complete IFB package is assembled, the procurement is then publicly announced in the hope of generating as much competition as possible. The public announcement usually takes the dual form of a newspaper advertisement and a notification sent to all prospective contractors on the bidder's list. The newspaper advertisement generally appears in the legal advertisement section. An example of a typical newspaper advertisement appears below.

**Example of a Public Announcement of an
Invitation for Bids
Notice to Bidders**

The Pinewood County Human Resources Department hereby solicits sealed bids for the provision of homemaker services to elderly and physically disabled individuals residing within the geographical limits of Canyon City. Bids will be received until 5:00 p.m. on June 23, 19XX at the offices of the Pinewood County Human Resource Department, 1335 N. 7th Street, Canyon City, at which time all bids will be publicly opened and a contract awarded to the responsible bidder submitting the lowest responsive bid. Copies of the invitation for bids package including full particulars can be secured by writing the Pinewood County Human Resources Department at the address listed above or by calling (602) 555-6789. A bidders' conference will be held at the offices of the Pinewood County Human Resources Department at 1:00 p.m. on June 17, 19XX. Prospective bidders who do not attend the bidder's conference do so at their own risk.

STEP 3: IFB PACKAGES DISTRIBUTED

Prospective contractors interested in providing the service simply contact the government contracting agency and request the IFB package. Often a government contracting agency will maintain a bidder's list. A bidder's list is simply a registry of all individuals and organizations that have requested to be notified when a particular service is to be procured. A bidder's list provides a simple method for government human service contracting agencies to ensure that prospective contractors do not miss an opportunity to bid on a service procurement. Bidder's list notices need to be nothing more elaborate than a copy of the legal advertisement sent to the prospective contractor's business address.

STEP 4: BIDDER'S CONFERENCE HELD

Open sharing of all information with all prospective contractors is an important principle in formal advertising. A bidder's conference is generally conducted by the government contracting agency to answer any questions prospective contractors may have about the procurement. A common practice is for minutes of the bidder's conference to be kept. A summary of all questions posed, and the responses provided, is sent to all prospective contractors that requested copies of the IFB package whether or not they attended the bidder's conference. This practice ensures that all prospective contractors have access to the same information regarding the procurement. An objective of formal advertising is to ensure that all prospective contractors are treated equally.

STEP 5: SUBMISSION, OPENING, AND RECORDING OF BIDS

Prospective contractors may submit their sealed bids up to the appointed time for bid opening. As a general rule late bids are not accepted. The bids are opened in a public meeting and recorded. Often prospective contractors will attend the bid opening and record their competitors' bids. This practice is considered proper and serves to promote competition in future procurements.

STEP 6: BIDS DETERMINED RESPONSIVE

Following the public opening and recording of the bids, each bid is reviewed for "responsiveness." The responsiveness test is critical from a legal standpoint because each bid must constitute a legal offer. A responsive bid can be defined as follows:

Definition of Responsive Bid

A bid that complies with the invitation for bids package in all material respects both as to the method of service provision and the substance of any resulting contract. (Office of Federal Procurement Policy, 1979).

If as part of its submitted bid, a prospective contractor takes exception to any part of the work statement or any of the contract terms and conditions, or if any type of counteroffer is made, then the bid does not constitute a legal offer. Bids determined to be nonresponsive are thrown out.

STEP 7: CONTRACTOR DETERMINED RESPONSIBLE

Contractor responsibility is the following determination:

Definition of Contractor Responsibility

The contractor has the requisite skills, financial resources, and business integrity to discharge the contract satisfactorily, or has the business integrity and can acquire the requisite skills and financial resources (General Services Administration, n.d.)

The determination of contractor responsibility is another area where legal considerations are important. In a responsibility determination, the government contracting agency is essentially saying either "yes," the prospective contractor appears capable of providing the service and carrying out the terms of the contract, or "no," the prospective contractor does not. When a government contracting agency believes a prospective contractor is "nonresponsible," the background information and documentation is usually turned over to legal counsel for guidance prior to any formal action being initiated. It's a very delicate area, because in a sense a prospective contractor is being denied the opportunity to prove itself, yet the government contracting agency is also bound to protect itself against agreeing to a contract that appears to have a high probability of failure.

STEP 8: CONTRACT AWARD

The final step in formal advertising is the awarding of the contract. At this point, the government contracting agency has determined which prospective contractor is the responsible bidder submitting the lowest responsive bid. Contrary to popular belief, formal advertising does not require that the contract always be awarded to the low bidder. The low bidder must also be responsible and must have submitted a responsive bid. If the low bidder is determined nonresponsible or if its bid is found to be nonresponsive, the contract is awarded to the responsible bidder submitting the second lowest responsive bid.

In summary, formal advertising is a highly structured process that makes no allowance for negotiation. Formal advertising requires a work statement so that prospective contractors know exactly what is expected and thus can price their services accordingly. Competition must be present so that market forces can be used to establish a fair price.

COMPETITIVE NEGOTIATION

Negotiation, as the term applies to contracting, means "the process of discussing and bargaining with a view to reaching an agreement" (Office of Federal Procurement Policy, 1979). Where competition is involved, the procurement is called "competitive negotiation." Competitive negotiation has been the most popular method of procurement in human services, and is generally associated with its procurement document—the request for proposals (RFP).

Competitive negotiation, or the request for proposal process, is the appropriate procurement to be used when either of the following conditions exists:

Conditions for Use of Competitive Negotiation

- Any of the three conditions necessary for formal advertising cannot be met.
- New or creative service delivery approaches are desired.

If adequate competition does not exist for the service to be procured, if price cannot be the major criterion in the award, or if a work statement does not exist, then formal advertising cannot be used and, by default, competitive negotiation must be used. Competitive negotiation is also indicated when the government contracting agency wishes to generate new or creative service delivery approaches from prospective contractors.

The major steps involved in competitive negotiations are essentially the same as the steps in formal advertising except for the following four differences: (1) a request for proposals package is prepared rather than an invitation for bids package; (2) a proposal evaluation step is required; (3) negotiations are conducted; and (4) contracts are awarded on the basis of the proposal that appears to meet the identified need most closely, price and other factors being considered.

A significant difference for the prospective contractor is that a proposal is written in which services to be provided can be described, thus offering the opportunity to compete for a contract on the basis of such factors as quality, creativity, service capacity, or ability to serve a special population. The negotiation step permits further elaboration on the prospective contractor's ability to meet the identified need.

The major steps in competitive negotiations are the following:

Steps in Competitive Negotiation
Step 1: RFP package prepared.
Step 2: Procurement advertised.
Step 3: RFP packages distributed.
Step 4: Proposer's conference held.
Step 5: Submission, opening, and recording of proposals conducted.
Step 6: Proposals evaluated.
Step 7: Proposals determined responsive.
Step 8: Contractor responsibility determined.
Step 9: Negotiations conducted.
Step 10: Contract awarded.

Under competitive negotiation, a public advertisement is needed, a proposer's conference is held, and proposals (either sealed or unsealed) are submitted, opened (if necessary), and recorded. Proposals, just like bids, are reviewed for responsiveness and the contractors determined responsible. Proposals submitted late are generally rejected.

Like IFB packages, RFP packages can take many different forms. Nevertheless, certain indentifiable elements appear in most RFP packages and there is a certain logical order to the arrangement. The outline depicted below represents a distillation of many human service and nonhuman service RFPs used by the federal government and various states, counties, and municipalities, and can be used to cover the vast majority of competitive procurements in POSC for human services.

OUTLINE OF A MODEL POSC
REQUEST FOR PROPOSAL

I. *TABLE OF CONTENTS*

A description of all sections of the RFP.

II. *GENERAL INFORMATION*

The name of the agency issuing the RFP (the government contracting agency).
The service(s) involved.
How to obtain copies of the RFP.
The date and time of the proposer's conference.

The proposal due date.
The number of proposal copies to be submitted.
The location for submission of proposals.
Acceptable mode of proposal submission (e.g., mail, certified mail, hand delivery).
The type and amount of funding involved (optional addition).

III. *PROPOSAL REVIEW SCHEDULE*

The date proposals will be reviewed.
The date and time for proposers to make oral presentations (optional addition).
How and when successful/unsuccessful proposers will be notified.
The target date for contract award.

IV. PROPOSAL EVALUATION CRITERIA

The evaluation criteria.
The relative value of each criterion.

V. WORK STATEMENT/PROPOSAL NARRATIVE

A. A work statement, and/or
B. A format to describe the proposed service delivery approach.

VI. SERVICE DELIVERY HISTORY, KEY STAFF QUALIFICATIONS, FACILITIES, AND EQUIPMENT

A format for the proposer to describe its service delivery history and key service staff qualifications, facilities, and equipment.

VII. PRICE QUOTES/BUDGET SECTION

A. A format for the proposer to enter price quotes, or
B. A detailed budget, budget justification narrative, and cost allocation plan (if required).

VIII. PROPOSAL SUBMITTAL LETTER

The legal name of the individual or organization submitting the proposal.
The contracting authority of the proposer (e.g., corporate charter or bylaws).
The proposer's contact person for negotiation purposes.

The signature of an individual legally empowered to submit the proposal on behalf of the proposer.

IX. PROPOSAL SUBMITTAL CHECKLIST

A list of all parts of the RFP package to be returned.
The desired order in which RFP sections are to be arranged.

An example of how the model outline can be applied to a request for proposals for homemaker services is contained in Appendix B.

A detailed discussion of the model POSC request for proposals outline is beyond the scope of this chapter. However, the rationale underlying certain elements of the model RFP should be made explicit. Section I, the Table of Contents, enables prospective contractors to check their copies for completeness. Section II, General Information, provides important dates and times, and often the type and amount of available funding is included. Although far from a settled argument, many human services POSC administrators believe that the inclusion of this information precludes wasted effort in the development of proposals too expensive to be funded.

The inclusion of Section III, Proposal Review Schedule, can save the government contracting agency a great deal of time that would otherwise be spent responding individually to such questions. If prospective contractors will be required to make oral presentations of their proposals, the date and time for the oral presentations should be included here.

Publishing Section IV, Proposal Evaluation Criteria, and their relative values requires that the government contracting agency determine ahead of time what factors other than price are important. This approach serves to establish an objective set of criteria and a system of weighting each criterion in accordance with its relative importance. This approach also provides the government contracting agency/evaluators with a buffer against external attempts to influence contracting decisions.

The inclusion of Section V, Work Statement and/or a Proposal Narrative, depends to a large extent on how much the government contracting agency knows about the service to be procured. If the government contracting agency is absolutely certain in all details about the service, then a detailed work statement is included in the RFP package and a minimal response by the proposer is required. If, however, the government contracting agency knows little about the service and is dependent upon the proposer to supply the details, or if the government contracting agency is attempting to stimulate creative responses to an identified problem or need, then two options are available: (1) the inclusion of a work statement that uses only performance specifications (see Chapter 4), or (2) the replacement of a work statement with an outline format that permits prospective contractors to describe their proposed service delivery approaches. Section VI, Service Delivery History, Key Staff Qualifications, Facilities, and Equipment, permits the proposer to describe the agency's capability to perform the service.

The use of Section VII, Price Quotes, or the inclusion of a Budget Section again depends upon the procurement objectives. When competition is not expected, a budget section becomes necessary so that a reasonable service price can be determined. A budget need not be a part of every proposal, however. When competition is expected and market forces can be used to establish a fair service price, the inclusion of a budget section is of questionable utility and can be eliminated in favor of price quotes. The homemaker RFP in Appendix B uses the price quotes approach.

Section VIII, The Proposal Submittal Letter, is designed with certain legal considerations in mind. This letter is used to establish the contracting authority of the proposer, secure a signature on the proposal, and identify a contact person for subsequent questions and negotiations. Section IX, The Proposal Submittal Checklist, identifies the portions of the RFP package that must be returned and in the desired order. This procedure aids in reviewing submitted proposals for responsiveness.

On receipt of a request for proposals, a prospective contractor should do the following:

- check it for completeness;
- take note of all general information, noting due dates on a calendar;
- record key proposal review dates on a calendar;
- assess evaluation criteria to understand where to place emphasis and to help estimate likelihood of success;
- analyze work statement as outlined in Chapter 4;
- plan who will write what sections of the proposal;
- plan who will develop the budget.

As with so many other projects, reading, interpreting, and preparing to respond to an RFP is much less imposing and more manageable when the work is shared and each person contributes from an area of strength.

After proposals have been submitted and evaluated, proposals determined to be in the competitive range are continued in the process and all others are eliminated. Each proposer is informed of weaknesses or deficiencies in the proposal and given an opportunity to make a "best and final offer." (Unlike formal advertising, under competitive negotiation the submission of a proposal is not deemed to constitute a legal offer. The submission of a proposal is considered nothing more than an expression of interest and an "invitation to dicker.") When each prospective contractor has made a best and final offer, the government contracting agency evaluates all offers, prioritizes its selections, and begins negotiations with the potential contractor who offers the contract most advantageous to the government contracting agency. This expression "most advantageous to the government contracting agency" appears often in federal government contracting literature and has been a subject of controversy among prospective contractors. It should be remembered, however, that the government contracting agency is charged with ensuring the best possible services for the greatest number of clients, and it is in this context that the term "advantageous" should be interpreted. When agreement is reached on all terms and conditions, a contract document is drawn up and signed.

TWO-STEP FORMAL ADVERTISING

Two-step formal advertising is the last of the three competitive procurements to be discussed. Two-step formal advertising combines formal advertising and competitive negotiation into one procurement. In so doing, it offers a unique method whereby market forces and competition can be combined with service quality safeguards.

Conditions for Use of Two-Step Formal Advertising

- Desire to introduce competition and infuse market forces into the procurement.
- Desire to ensure service quality through the use of nonprice decision criteria.

The two steps referred to in two-step formal advertising are as follows:

Steps in Two-Step Formal Advertising

Step 1: The issuance of a request for proposals, the purpose of which is to

> determine the suitability of potential contractors and their service delivery methodologies.
>
> Step 2: The issuance of an invitation for bids to all potential contractors determined suitable and contract award to the lowest responsible bidder submitting a responsive bid.

The first step consists of the issuance of an RFP. The government contracting agency enumerates as many service quality standards and prospective contractor qualifications as are deemed appropriate. No information on cost or price is solicited at this time. When submitted proposals are evaluated, they are divided into three categories: (1) acceptable as submitted, (2) acceptable with minor modifications, and (3) not acceptable. Negotiations are entered into with the proposers in category (2) whose proposals are acceptable, with minor modifications needed to correct the deficiencies. The request for proposals process is handled in exactly the same manner as competitive negotiations.

During step two , an invitation for bids is issued to those prospective contractors whose proposals were acceptable and those whose proposals were corrected and made acceptable. The IFB process is conducted in exactly the same manner as formal advertising and the contract is awarded to the responsible prospective contractor submitting the lowest responsive bid.

SOLE-SOURCE

Because of its technical requirements, sole-source procurement does not generally apply to POSC for human services. Sole-source procurement as a concept came about because of patents, trademarks, copyrights, and single distributorships. When only one business can supply a product or piece of equipment because it holds the patent, trademark, or copyright (or is the single representative of the business that does), no amount of competition will alter this fact.

The application of the concept of sole-source to POSC for human services is of questionable validity. Typically human services are not patented, trademarked, or copyrighted. All too frequently, however, the contention is made that when only one human service organization exists in a given city, county, or region, a government contracting agency is justified in using a sole-source procurement. In situations in which only one prospective contractor is known to exist, competitive negotiation, not sole-source, should be used. If only one prospective contractor competes for the contract, no harm has been done. However,

PROCUREMENT

a government contracting agency may well discover, through the use of competitive negotiation, that an existing agency in another area would be willing to start a satellite operation, that a group of concerned citizens might form a new nonprofit organization to compete for the contract, or that an existing proprietary agency might consider providing the service. Competition and market forces can be used to create new prospective contractors or to redirect the thinking of existing nonprofit and proprietary organizations.

PROCUREMENT AND THE PARTNERSHIP/MARKET CONTINUUM

Figure 5.2 illustrates where formal advertising, competitive negotiation, and two-step formal advertising fall on the partnership/market continuum. Competitive negotiation is the procurement closest to the partnership end of the continuum. Formal advertising is closest to the market end. As might be expected, two-step formal advertising falls in the middle.

More and more government contracting agencies today are concerned with infusing competition and market forces into their POSC activities. However, many feel that formal advertising would be too radical a transition for themselves and their contractors. Consequently they continue using competitive negotiation. An incremental move in the direction of the market model would be the adoption of two-step formal advertising for some selected services. Because two-step formal advertising begins with a request for proposals and then bridges into an invitation for bids, this procurement represents a natural method by which government contracting agencies can test the usefulness of formal advertising for their contractors and themselves.

SUMMARY

- Three procurement processes suitable for use in the human services are formal advertising, competitive negotiation, and two-step formal advertising.
- Formal advertising should be the procurement of choice when a government contracting agency (1) knows precisely what it wants to purchase, (2) has developed a work statement, and (3) anticipates adequate competition.
- Competitive negotiation should be used when a government contracting agency is confronted by any one of the following: (1) absence of competition, (2) the lack of a work statement, (3) the desire to consider factors other than price in contract award, (4) the desire to have prospective contractors propose new or creative service delivery methods.

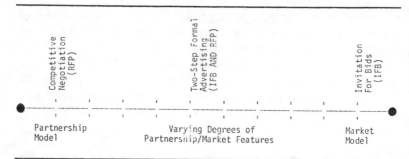

Figure 5.2: An illustration of where different procurements fall on the partnership/
market continuum.

- Two-step formal advertising combines the flexibility of competitive negotiation with the generation of competition and infusion of market forces created by the use of formal advertising. Two-step formal advertising can also be used as a bridge, or intermediate step, for a government contracting agency that wants to move away from the partnership model of POSC and toward the market model.
- Sole-source is usually an inappropriate procurement to use in POSC for human services unless a patent, trademark, or copyright is involved.

EXERCISE:
DETERMINING TYPES OF PROCUREMENTS

Indicate the type of procurement (IFB, RFP, two-step, or sole-source)
you would use in each of the following situations.

Procurement

_____   (1) The provision of bookkeeper classroom training is required. Training is to be provided to a minimum of 25 and a maximum of 35 economically disadvantaged female heads of household.

_____   (2) Child day-care services are required for approximately 2,000 children countywide to be provided 5 days per week for a period of one year.

_____   (3) A second-year evaluation of a home-care case management unit is required. The evaluation is to utilize the methodology developed and used the previous year by Western Consultants, Inc.

_____   (4) Transportation services are desired to transport up to 20 senior citizens Monday through Friday, excluding holidays, to and from the Sunnyside Senior Center. The senior citizens all live within a five-mile radius of the Sunnyside Senior Center.

_____ (5) Homemaker services are desired for 50 elderly and physically disabled individuals residing within Lakeside County. It is anticipated that approximately 10,000 units of service will be required during the twelve-month term of the contract with one unit of service being one hour of actual service delivery time exclusive of travel time to and from clients' residences.

EXERCISE ANSWERS:
DETERMINING TYPES OF PROCUREMENT

1. The provision of bookkeeper classroom training is required. Training is to be provided to a minimum of 25 and a maximum of 35 economically disadvantaged female heads of household.

An RFP would most likely be used in this situation unless the government contracting agency has developed and used a work statement for bookkeeper training services and is confident enough in it to go out for bids. A two-step process would be a second choice. In Step 1, an RFP could be issued for a training package. Those prospective contractors whose training packages are found acceptable could then submit a bid on the contract during step 2.

2. Child day-care services are required for approximately 2,000 children countywide to be provided 5 days per week for a period of one year.

An IFB could be used in this situation. Most states regulate child day-care centers. Consequently, service standards exist and could be translated into a work statement. Adequate competition should not be a problem because of the large number of proprietary day-care centers operating in most parts of the country. Clearly, however, this will depend on the local community.

3. A second-year evaluation of a home-care case management unit is requested. The evaluation is to utilize the methodology developed and used the previous year by Western Consultants, Inc.

If Western Consultants, Inc., holds the copyright to the evaluation methodology, this may be a case for a sole-contract. If the evaluation is not copyrighted, the methodology could be used to develop a work statement and an IFB utilized.

4. Transportation services are required to transport up to 20 senior

citizens Monday through Friday, excluding holidays, to and from the Sunnyside Senior Center. The senior citizens all live within a five-mile radius of the Sunnyside Senior Center.

Transportation is one area where good work statements have been developed. Additionally, securing competition should not be a problem. Consequently, an IFB could be used here quite effectively.

5. Homemaker services are desired for 50 elderly and physically disabled individuals residing within Lakeside County. It is anticipated that approximately 10,000 units of service will be required during the twelve-month term of the contract with one unit of service being one hour of actual service delivery time exclusive of travel time to and from clients' residences.

Homemaker services is also an area where some good work statements have been developed. There are also a large number of proprietary contractors providing homemaker services so securing competition should not be a problem. An IFB should work well in this situation.

COMMENTS ON EXERCISE

It should be obvious from the exercise that the selection of a procurement is largely dependent upon the existence of a work statement. Due to the general lack of work statements in POSC, most government contracting agencies would probably use an RFP for the majority of the service situations in this exercise, even though other options might serve them better.

Chapter 6

PRICE AND COST ANALYSIS

What is a fair price? What is a reasonable price? Suppose you are in the market for a new refrigerator. You identify the features important to you and then watch ads in the newspaper. You find the cheapest, the most expensive, and several in between. When you find the lowest-priced refrigerator that has all the features you want, you have arrived at a fair price.

Now suppose you have inherited a rare oriental rug. You wish to sell it and you don't want to get cheated, but neither do you want to keep it in storage for several years. It is not likely that there will be competition so you have to establish the price in a different way. You evaluate rugs similar to yours, perhaps get yours appraised, and arrive at a figure you feel comfortable with. You have now established, in POSC terms, a reasonable price.

Price theory states that when adequate competition is present in a procurement, the emphasis of the financial review is on the establishment of a *fair price*. When adequate competition is not present in a procurement, price theory states that the emphasis of the financial review should be on the establishment of a *reasonable price*.

The Principles of Price Theory

- When adequate competition is present in a procurement, the objective of the financial review is to establish a fair price.
- When adequate competition is not present in a procurement, the objective of the financial review is to establish a reasonable price.

ADEQUATE COMPETITION

In describing price and cost analysis we will establish two sets of relationships:

adequate competition ⟶ fair price ⟶ no price and cost
analysis required

and

no adequate competition ⟶ reasonable price ⟶ price and cost
analysis required

But first let's look at a case example that illustrates the importance of carefully calculating costs.

THE CASE OF MISCALCULATED COSTS

A family counseling agency noticed in the paper a request for proposals to provide family counseling services to families of abused and neglected children. They put together a proposal, and when it came to calculating the budget, tried to itemize all of their costs. They included an additional staff person, employee-related expenses, mileage, a new desk and office furniture and, equipment. Because the agency was already in operation, they did not include such expenses as rent and utilities, or administrative and clerical staff costs. When their proposal was evaluated, their unit cost was the lowest and, because they were determined to be "responsible," they got the contract.

Once the program began operating, it took a great deal of the executive director's time as well as that of the clerical staff. A budding program on group counseling for adolescents suffered from lack of administrative attention and had to be discontinued. Reports to the Board went uncompleted. A Board investigation was initiated. Ultimately the problems were traced to the heavy demands placed on the agency by the new program.

Often agencies submitting proposals fail to recognize the importance of listing all their costs—both direct and indirect. This chapter will illustrate methods for calculating the exact costs of providing a service.

ADEQUATE COMPETITION/FAIR PRICE/PRICE AND COSTS ANALYSIS NOT REQUIRED

The federal government has set forth four criteria for use in determining whether or not adequate competition is present in a procurement (Office of Federal Procurement Policy, 1980). First, there must be at least two prospective contractors. Second, they must be "responsible" prospective contractors within the meaning of that term as defined in Chapter 5 and be willing to provide service as specified in the work statement. Third, the prospective contractors must have acted independently in the preparation and submission of their bids or proposals—a test for noncollusion. Finally, they must have submitted responsive bids or proposals within the meaning of that term as defined in Chapter 5.

The Test for Adequacy of Competition

At least two responsible bidders or proposers submitting responsive and independently developed bids or proposals.

FAIR PRICE

The principle used to determine a fair price is that in situations of perfect (or near perfect) competition the marketplace can be used to determine the price a government contracting agency should pay for a service. According to price theory, a fair price is taken to mean the market price, which as a practical matter is the lowest price. It is price theory that provides the normative basis for the use of formal advertising and the awarding of POSC contracts to the lowest bidder when adequate competition is present and all other evaluative factors are equal. This is important for prospective contractors to understand because no analysis will be conducted and services will be contracted for the price quoted. If that price is $1 per year, it will be expected that services will be delivered for that price.

Fair Price

Where competition is present, a fair price is established by the market:
Fair Price = Market Price = Low Bid or Proposal

When adequate competition is absent from a procurement, price and cost analysis are used to establish a reasonable price, as spelled out in detail in the following section.

A DECISION MATRIX FOR CONDUCTING A PRICE AND COST ANALYSIS

The Federal government has developed a decision matrix for federal government contract officials to use in conducting a price and cost analysis (Office of Federal Procurement Policy, 1980). The decision matrix, slightly altered for use in POSC for human services, is illustrated in Figure 6.1. The illustration is intended to provide a framework for thinking through the issues in price and cost analysis, not as a model directly applicable to POSC in human services.

The decision matrix poses the following questions:

Question 1. "Is there adequate competition?" If the answer is yes, the financial review can be considered complete and the contract awarded to the lowest bidder or proposer. If the answer is no, the analysis proceeds to Question 2.

Question 2. "Is the price reasonable compared to market prices?" How does this price compare to prices being paid for the same or similar services by the government contracting agency? If the price is considered

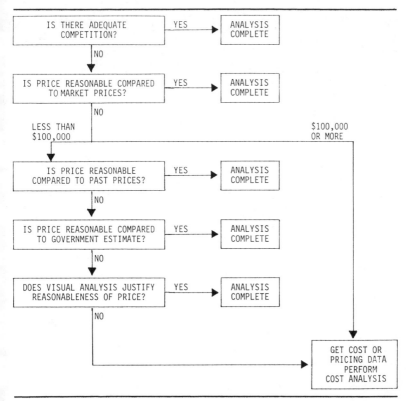

Figure 6.1: Price and cost analysis.

reasonable, the analysis can be considered complete. If it is not, the analysis divides into two branches.

If the estimated cost of service provision is $100,000 or more, a cost analysis is performed. This involves an analysis of the cost and pricing data (budgetary data) submitted by the prospective contractors in support of their bids or proposals. Following the analysis a final price is negotiated.

If the estimated cost of service provision is under $100,000, the analysis proceeds to Question 3.

Question 3. "Is the price reasonable compared to past prices?" Has the government contracting agency previously paid a similar price for the same or a similar service? If the answer is yes, the analysis can be considered complete. If the answer is no, the analysis proceeds to Question 4.

Question 4. "Is the price reasonable compared to estimates?" A government contracting agency may have estimated the cost of the service prior to conducting the procurement. If the price is considered reasonable compared to these estimates, the analysis can be considered complete. If it is not considered reasonable, the analysis proceeds to Question 5.

Question 5. "Does a visual analysis justify the reasonableness of the price?" If no formal estimates were made, an informal calculation may be undertaken at this point. Informal calculation simply involves a checking of budget figures and a judgment on the part of the reviewer that the price is reasonable based on the information available. If the answer is yes, the analysis can be considered complete. If the answer is no, the financial review should take the approach of a cost analysis of the prospective contractor's cost and pricing data.

PRICE ANALYSIS

Price analysis can be defined as follows:

Definition of Price Analysis

The process of examining and evaluating a prospective contractor's price without evaluating cost or pricing data or proposed profit, if any. (U.S. General Accounting Office, 1980)

This means that answers to questions 2, 3, 4, and 5 will be pursued without evaluating cost and pricing data or proposed profit. Cost and pricing data can be equated with any budgetary information submitted in support of a bid or proposal.

A CONTRACTOR'S PROFIT MARGIN

Proprietary (for-profit) agencies are allowed to compete and contract with the government for provision of human services. Many human service professionals are philosophically opposed to this. However, from the government contracting agency perspective, overriding criteria must always be the best possible service for the lowest possible price. Although a number of studies have been undertaken over the years, there appear to be no definitive answers about the superiority of for-profit versus nonprofit agencies. In a recent survey of 43 state POSC administrators, no significant differences were found in the perceived quality of POSC services delivered by for-profit and nonprofit contractors (Martin, 1986).

A second consideration is the many costs absorbed by nonprofit agencies, and the implications of this for the future of POSC. Anthony and Hertzlinger (1975) argue that nonprofit agencies seldom figure (or in some instances may be precluded from figuring) into their cost of service provision their true costs for such items as depreciation and the cost of working capital. They suggest that nonprofit agencies should be allowed to earn a profit on the services they deliver as a method of recovering "unmeasured costs." Such a practice would also enable nonprofits to grow in size and capability, a factor that might be of some importance to government contracting agencies pursuing a partnership approach to POSC.

COST ANALYSIS

When adequate competition is not present in a procurement, or when price analysis has failed to establish a fair price, cost analysis is used. Cost analysis has been defined as follows:

Definition of Cost Analysis

The process of reviewing and evaluating a prospective contractor's cost and pricing data and the judgment used by the prospective contractor in projecting from the data to the estimated contract cost. (U.S. General Accounting Office, 1980)

Cost analysis consists of a financial review of budgetary information supplied by prospective contractors in support of their bids or proposals. The financial review generally takes the form of applying tests to each cost item. These four tests are designed to determine the following:

Cost Analysis Tests in POSC For Human Services

- The necessity of the cost.
- The reasonableness of the cost.
- The allowability of the cost.
- The allocability of the cost.

Applying these tests calls for additional data collection, study, and use of judgment by the reviewers.

THE NECESSITY OF THE COST

Not every cost item that a prospective contractor may build into a service budget plan may actually need to be a part of the service. Take, for example, the following hypothetical situation involving a POSC procurement for home-delivered meals. One prospective contractor has included costs for a half-time dietician in their budgetary data. The POSC work statement stipulated that "the contractor shall utilize three-week cycle menus developed by the government contracting agency's registered dietician." The half-time dietician is unnecessary in this instance. When a cost item cannot pass the test of necessity, it is disallowed.

THE REASONABLENESS OF THE COST

The reasonableness test is often referred to as the "prudent person test." Would a prudent person spend the amount of money proposed by the prospective contractor on the cost item under consideration? Continuing with the home-delivered meals example, suppose the budgetary data proposed a half-time cook's salary at an annual cost of $8,500. Does this amount seem reasonable and would a prudent person pay this amount? The answer is most likely "yes" in this situation given the nature of the work and pay scale for cooks. However, when a cost item cannot pass the test of reasonableness, it is disallowed.

THE ALLOWABILITY OF THE COST

The test for allowability is required because a cost item allowable under one set of cost principles may be unallowable under another. This phenomenon is primarily associated with the use of federal funds. However, many state and local governments have developed cost principles of their own. The cost principles of the U.S. Department of Health and Human Services serve to illustrate the issue of allowability. The Department's cost principles are set forth in Chapter 45, *Code of Federal Regulations*, Part 74. There is a different set of cost principles for each of the following: state and local governments, educational institutions, research and development contracts and grants with hospitals, nonprofit organizations, and for-profit organizations.

Many cost items are uniformly allowable or unallowable across the varying sets of cost principles; some are not. Consequently, prudent financial reviewers working on POSC contracts want to be very familiar with the differences. When a cost item cannot pass the test of allowability, it is disallowed.

THE ALLOCABILITY OF THE COST

The test for allocability is necessary because indirect costs should not simply be charged off entirely against any one program or service. Generally accepted accounting principles require that indirect costs be allocated according to some formula or plan. When a cost item represents an indirect cost and the item has not been allocated, it is disallowed.

Cost allocation, the name given to the process of distributing indirect costs, is a complex undertaking best left to the accountants. However, the theory of cost allocation is not difficult and is fundamental to a complete understanding of cost analysis. The remainder of this chapter and the exercise that follows are designed to acquaint the reader with the concepts of direct and indirect costs and cost allocation.

DIRECT COSTS, INDIRECT COSTS, AND COST ALLOCATION

Costs are generally classified as either direct or indirect. A direct cost is assignable to (i.e., directly benefits) only one program. Examples of direct costs include the following:

Examples of Direct Costs

- salaries of personnel who work exclusively on one program or service;
- materials and other supplies used exclusively for one pogram or service;
- travel costs associated with one program or service;
- equipment used exclusively for one program or service

An indirect cost is assignable to more than one program. Indirect costs are typically involved with some general support operation that benefits all programs of the agency. As a result, indirect costs are sometimes referred to as "agency overhead costs." Examples of indirect costs include the following:

Examples of Indirect Costs

- the agency director's salary
- the salary of the business manager, accountants, and bookkeepers
- building rents
- utilities and janitorial services

- legal and audit costs
- telephone, supplies, postage, and reproduction.

To ensure that each program pays its proper share, indirect costs are divided among all of the programs using cost allocation. Three different methods of cost allocation can be used and are generally acceptable. Indirect costs can be allocated by (1) calculating each program's percentage of total direct costs; (2) calculating each program's percentage of personnel related costs; or (3) converting indirect costs into direct costs.

CALCULATING EACH PROGRAM'S PERCENTAGE OF TOTAL DIRECT COSTS

Each program operating within an agency will have direct costs assigned for those personnel and operating expenses incurred exclusively within that program. Totaling all direct costs for each program will provide a figure for Total Direct Costs. These figures are used to calculate each program's percentage of total costs, as illustrated in the following example of an agency with three programs:

Step 1. All agency cost items in its budget are separated into four categories: direct costs assignable to programs 1, 2, and 3, and indirect costs.

	Program 1	Program 2	Program 3	Indirect Costs
Salaries and Wages				
Director				25,000
Supervisors	20,000	20,000	20,000	
Social workers	35,000	42,000	18,000	
Secretaries				30,000
Operations				
Equipment				15,000
Rent				12,000
Utilities				2,400
Travel				
In state	2,000	3,000	1,500	
Out of state	1,000	1,500	750	

Step 2. All costs in each of the four categories are totaled.

	Program 1	Program 2	Program 3	Indirect Costs
Total	$58,000	$66,500	$40,250	$84,400

Step 3. The totaled costs for each of the three services are themselves totaled. The sum of all direct program costs is called the agency's "total direct costs."

	Program 1		Program 2		Program 3		Total Direct Costs
Totals	$58,000	+	$66,500	+	$40,250	=	$164,750

Step 4. The totaled costs for each of the three programs are divided by the agency's total direct costs, thus generating a percentage figure that represents each program's relative percentage share of the agency's total direct costs.

Program 1	Program 2	Program 3
$\dfrac{58,000}{\$164,750} = 35.2\%$	$\dfrac{66,500}{\$164,750} = 40.4\%$	$\dfrac{40,250}{\$164,750} = 24.4\%$

Step 5. Each of the three program's percentages is then applied to the total indirect costs.

Program 1	Program 2	Program 3
$84,400	$84,400	$84,400
× .352	× .404	× .244
$29,708.80	$34,097.60	$20,593.60

Step 6. Each program's direct costs and its percentage of indirect costs are totaled. The sum of a program's direct and indirect costs is called the "total program costs."

	Program 1	Program 2	Program 3
Direct costs	$58,000	$ 66,500	$40,250
Indirect costs	$29,708.80	$ 34,097.60	$20,593.60
Total program costs	$87,708.80	$100,587.60	$60,843.60

The following example puts all of the foregoing pieces together into a graphic depiction of a cost allocation plan using total direct costs:

Examples of a Cost Allocation Plan Using Total Direct Costs

	Program 1	Program 2	Program 3	Indirect Costs
Salaries and Wages				
Executive director				$25,000
Supervisors	$20,000	$20,000	$20,000	
Social workers	$35,000	$42,000	$18,000	
Secretaries				$30,000
Operations				
Equipment				$15,000
Rent				$12,000
Utilities				$ 2,400
Travel				
In state	$ 2,000	$ 3,000	$ 1,500	
Out of state	$ 1,000	$ 1,500	$ 750	
TOTAL DIRECT COSTS	$58,000	$66,500	$40,250	
	35.2%	40.4%	24.4%	
TOTAL INDIRECT COSTS				$84,400
ALLOCATION OF INDIRECT COSTS	$29,708.80	$34,097.60	$20,593.60	
TOTAL PROGRAM COSTS	$87,708.80	$100,597.60	$60,843.60	

CALCULATING EACH PROGRAM'S PERCENTAGE OF PERSONNEL-RELATED COSTS

Allocating costs using each program's share of personnel is done in the same manner as the previous example with the following exceptions:

At Step 2, only personnel costs (salaries, wages, and fringe benefits) are totaled.

Program 1	Program 2	Program 3
$55,000	$62,000	$38,000

At Step 3, personnel costs for each program are totaled to determine total personnel costs.

Program 1		Program 2		Program 3	
$55,000	+	$62,000	+	$38,000 = $155,000	

At Step 4, total personnel costs for each program are divided by total personnel costs for the agency. The result represents each program's share of total agency personnel costs.

Program 1	Program 2	Program 3
$\frac{\$\ 55,000}{\$155,000} = 35.5\%$	$\frac{\$\ 62,000}{\$155,000} = 40\%$	$\frac{\$\ 38,000}{\$155,000} = 24.5\%$

At Step 5, the percentages calculated are applied to total indirect costs.

Program 1	Program 2	Program 3
$84,400	$84,400	$84,400
× .355	× .40	× .245
$29,962	$33,760	$20,678

Step 6 is the same.

	Program 1	Program 2	Program 2
Direct costs	$58,000	$ 66,500	$40,250
Indirect costs	$29,962	$ 33,760	$20,678
Total program costs	$87,962	$100,260	$60,928

In this example, using personnel costs did not cause the total program costs to vary much because personnel costs and other operating costs are equally distributed across programs. However, if one or more program budget is heavily weighted toward personnel costs, the method of calculating indirect costs can make a significant difference.

CONVERTING INDIRECT COSTS INTO DIRECT COSTS

Still another method of dealing with indirect costs is to convert them into direct costs. In this approach, an allocation base is adopted for each indirect cost item. The base used is some measure of the work accomplished as a result of the incurrence of the indirect cost. For example, personnel offices are typically considered indirect costs. The costs of maintaining an agency's personnel function indirectly benefits all programs and services of an agency. An allocation base that could be used is the total number of agency employees. If an agency has 100 total employees and its family counseling program has ten of these employees, the family counseling program would be directly charged 10% of the costs of maintaining the personnel function. An agency that opts to convert all its indirect costs to direct costs does not need to go through the process of developing a cost allocation plan.

There are generally accepted allocation bases for converting most indirect cost items into direct costs. The following are selected examples of allocation bases suggested by the federal government:

Federally Suggested Allocation Bases	
Activity	Suggested Bases for Allocation
Accounting	Number of transactions processed
Auditing	Direct audit hours
Budgeting	Direct hours of identifiable services of employees of central budget
Data processing	System usage
Disbursing service	Number of checks or warrants issued
Legal services	Direct hours
Office space use and related costs (heat, light, janitor services, etc.)	Sq. ft. of space occupied

Organization and management services	Direct hours
Payroll services	Number of employees
Personnel administration	Number of employees
Printing and reproduction	Direct hours, job basis, pages printed
Procurement service	Number of transactions processed

WHICH COST ALLOCATION METHOD IS BEST?

There is no one best cost allocation method. Cost allocation requires knowledge, skill, and experience. Often, to the experienced eye, scanning the budget will help determine the best cost allocation method for the proposal under consideration. Of the three methods, each has its strengths and weaknesses depending on the type of program and the items in the budget.

One of the most important factors to look for in preparing or analyzing a budget is the extent to which indirect costs are spread across all programs. If a particular item or category of items tends to skew the budget significantly, then the cost allocation method should be selected carefully. One of the reasons that a special formula is allowed for personnel-related costs is that staff generally use more of the kind of resources covered in indirect costs than other budgeted items. For example, two programs within one agency might each have a budget of $100,000. One program, a counseling program, employs 5 professional staff and a secretary with a personnel budget of $90,000. The other, a congregate meal program, employs a cook and a dishwasher, and spends $70,000 a year for food. This would be an example where allocation based on total direct costs would result in allocating indirect costs very differently than would personnel related costs. Generally speaking, human service programs tend to be "labor intensive," and should be analyzed carefully for the impact of personnel on the total budget.

Allocation by converting indirect costs into direct costs is a sound and time-tested method for allocating direct costs, and in many cases it is the most equitable of the three methods. Its drawback, however, is that it is time consuming to track down the data needed to convert each indirect cost item into a direct cost.

WHY IS COST ALLOCATION IMPORTANT?

After looking at the complexity of cost allocation, one may be tempted to ask, "Why bother?" The reason is that accurate calculation of program costs is important in the POSC process. Each year decisions must be made about requests to start up new programs, terminate existing programs, expand, or cut back. Invariably a critical factor in these decisions will be the factor of unit costs. Unit costs are calculated by taking the total program costs and dividing them by the number of units of service provided. If the total program cost figure is not accurate because of poor cost allocation practices, the unit cost figure will not be accurate. If these figures are not reliable, it is entirely possible that the future of a particular program could be jeopardized because of a decision made during the cost allocation process.

SUMMARY

- Price theory states that when adequate competition is present in a procurement, the objective of the financial review is the establishment of a fair price; when adequate competition is not present, the objective is the establishment of a reasonable price.
- Price and cost analysis is the method by which a reasonable price is determined.
- Price analysis is the process of examining and evaluating a prospective contractor's price without evaluating cost or pricing data or proposed profit, if any.
- Cost analysis is the process of reviewing and evaluating a prospective contractor's cost and pricing data and the judgment used by the prospective contractor in projecting from the data to the estimated contract cost.
- There are three acceptable methods of cost allocation: (1) calculating each program's percentage of total direct costs; (2) calculating each program's share of personnel costs; and (3) converting indirect costs into direct costs.
- Cost allocation is important because it affects total program costs, unit costs and, ultimately, decisions about the future of the program.

COST ALLOCATION PLAN EXERCISE

The North Pleasantville Senior Center (NPSC) must submit budgetary information in support of its proposal to the Lakeside County Department of Human Services. The NPSC provides two services:

congregate nutrition services and socialization and recreation services. You are the executive director. As the executive director, the task has fallen to you to allocate your agency's indirect costs using "total direct costs" as your base. Exhibit A is your annual budget. Exibit B is the cost allocation plan format you must use. Exhibit C presents the answers.

EXHIBIT A

NORTH PLEASANTVILLE SENIOR CENTER (NPSC)
ANNUAL BUDGET

I. PERSONNEL $84,500.00

A. Director	$18,500.00	
B. Social worker	14,500.00*	
C. Business manager	16,000.00	
D. Recreation aid	10,000.00	
E. Janitor	7,500.00	
F. Cook	9,500.00	
G. Van driver	8,500.00**	
	$84,500.00	

II. EQUIPMENT . . . . $ 5,000.00**

(Depreciation on 15-passenger van,
useful life 3 years, acquisition
cost of $15,000.00)

III. OTHER OPERATING $94,050.00

A. Utilities	$ 4,200.00
B. Insurance (van)	400.00**
C. Insurance (building)	2,000.00
D. Supplies (office)	750.00
E. Supplies (food service)	1,000.00
F. Supplies (recreation)	4,500.00
G. Xerox	80,000.00
H. Food	1,200.00
	$94,050.00

TOTAL BUDGET $183,550.00

*The social worker works only in the socialization and recreation program.
**Transportation is defined as a socialization and recreation service.

EXHIBIT B
COST ALLOCATION PLAN

Budget Line Item	Congregate Meals	Socialization and Recreation	Indirect Costs
I. PERSONNEL			
A. Director			
B. Social worker			
C. Business manager			
D. Recreation aide			
E. Janitor			
F. Cook			
G. Van driver			
II. EQUIPMENT			
III. Other Operating			
A. Utilities			
B. Insurance (van)			
C. Insurance (building)			
D. Supplies (office)			
E. Supplies (recreation)			
F. Supplies (food service)			
G. Food			
H. Xerox			
Total Direct Costs			
Allocate Indirect Costs			TOTAL INDIRECT COSTS
Total Direct and Indirect Costs			

EXHIBIT C
COST ALLOCATION PLAN

Budget Line Item	Congregate Meals	Socialization and Recreation	Indirect Costs
I. PERSONNEL			
A. Director			18,500
B. Social worker		14,500	
C. Business manager			16,000
D. Recreation aide		10,000	
E. Janitor			7,500
F. Cook	9,500		
G. Van driver		8,500	
II. EQUIPMENT		5,000	
III. Other Operating			
A. Utilities			4,200
B. Insurance (van)		400	
C. Insurance (building)			2,000
D. Supplies (office)			750
E. Supplies (recreation)		1,000	
F. Supplies (food service)	4,500		
G. Food	80,000		
H. Xerox			1,200
Total Direct Costs	94,000 (70.5%)	39,400 (29.5%)	50,150
Allocate Indirect Costs	35,356	14,794	TOTAL INDIRECT COSTS
Total Direct and Indirect Costs	129,356	54,194	

Chapter 7

NEGOTIATION

OBJECTIVES

After completing this chapter, the reader will be able to:

- Define the following key concepts:
  - technical negotiations
  - business negotiations
  - assumptions
  - issues
  - settlement range
  - least acceptable result
  - maximum supportable position
  - overlap in settlement ranges
  - win-win negotiations
  - principled negotiation

- Discuss or explain the following:
  - the difference between negotiating in POSC and negotiating for the purchase of a product
  - the difference between technical and business issues for negotiation
  - the negotiation process
  - alternative styles of negotiation

- Perform the following function:
  - given a negotiation scenario, identify issues for negotiation and develop a proposed settlement range for each issue.

Much of the literature on the subject of negotiation leaves the impression that negotiation is a game in which one uses the skills of shrewdness, cunning, and craftiness to win. Consider, for example, the titles of some of the popular literature on the subject: *Negotiation. The Art of Getting What You Want* (Schatzki, 1981); *You Can Negotiate Anything* (Cohen, 1980) with this claim on the cover: "The World's Best Negotiator Tells You How to Get What You Want"; or *Negotiating Tactics: Bargain Your Way to Winning* (Levin, 1980). Although the content of these books generally advocates a reasoned approach, one is, nevertheless, left with the impression that the best negotiators are "Winners."

Within the context of POSC, however, negotiation takes on a different meaning. Winning is not necessarily the goal if it comes at the expense of the other side losing. The government contracting agency has the responsibility to serve a client population, and has elected to accomplish this through POSC rather than direct service delivery. Clearly, then, it is not in the interest of the government contracting agency to negotiate a contract for a price so low that the contractor cannot possibly meet minimum standards.

In a similar vein, the potential contractor in negotiation focuses not so much on winning as on negotiating the contract that will allow for provision of good quality services to clients while at the same time recognizing that the government contracting agency has obligations that extend far beyond the limits of this contract. The potential contractor must bear in mind that most government contracts have a cancellation clause, and a contract that appears not to be providing a good return on the investment of government dollars can be canceled. Second, the potential contractor must also bear in mind that he or she will be sitting across the table from government contracting agency negotiators next year, and will be in a much better negotiating position if past sessions have been negotiated with integrity.

In negotiating the purchase of a home or a car, the critical difference is that the negotiated item remains essentially the same regardless of price, so it is to the buyer's advantage to purchase for the lowest possible price. Not so in human services. If a service is purchased for the lowest possible price, negotiated by exercising the full power of the government contracting agency, it is likely that those who will suffer the consequences of an inadequately funded program will be clients. On the other hand, the government contracting agency has an obligation to stretch resources to serve as many people as possible, so extracting the maximum dollar figure is not necessarily the goal of the potential contractor. Rather, the goal of negotiations in POSC is to provide the highest volume and best quality of services at the lowest possible cost under conditions mutually satisfactory to the government contracting agency and the contractor.

PROPOSAL EVALUATION

Because contract negotiations are time-consuming (and therefore costly), it is in the interest of both the government contracting agency and prospective contractors to limit negotiations to competitive proposals where both parties have an interest in reaching agreement on the terms and conditions of a contract. Selecting proposals to be negotiated is accomplished in the proposal evaluation phase of the POSC process. Prospective contractors are well advised to pay careful attention to evaluation principles and criteria. It often happens that prospective contractors get so caught up in enthusiasm about their proposed project design that they are certain that evaluators will share in their enthusiasm. Evaluators, on the other hand, are instructed to stick strictly to the established criteria.

Selecting the best proposals involves both a technical and a business analysis and evaluation (USDHEW, 1971). Each of these parts of the proposal is analyzed in accordance with certain principles and evaluation criteria.

TECHNICAL EVALUATION

In selecting the proposals to be negotiated, certain principles are followed in conducting the technical evaluation. First and foremost, the proposal must be evaluated in accordance with the evaluation criteria contained in the RFP. New criteria or afterthoughts may not be introduced at this point. Although it is the intent that contracts should result in provision of the best possible service, awards should not be made on the basis of capabilities that exceed those needed for successful performance of the work.

Technical evaluation generally should be based on the following types of considerations:

**Considerations in the Technical Evaluation
of Proposals**

• The contractor's understanding of the scope of work as shown by the proposed service delivery approach

- Availability and competence of specific types of experienced personnel
- Availability of necessary facilities and/or equipment
- Innovative approaches, where appropriate
- Proposed method of assuring that work will be completed on time at an acceptable level of performance
- Reasonableness of proposed time frames
- Appropriateness of staff classification
- Necessity for resources requested
- Necessity for proposed travel
- Appropriateness of proposed subcontracting

The technical evaluation focuses on the strengths and weaknesses of the proposed design for delivery of service. Findings and recommendations must be supported with concrete technical data and documented for use in selection of the sources for negotiation and award.

The best advice for prospective contractors interested in increasing the likelihood of a positive technical evaluation is to place heavy emphasis on understanding and integrating the elements of the work statement as covered in Chapter 4. By analyzing programs in terms of inputs, throughputs, outputs, and outcomes, it is possible to identify weaknesses and inconsistencies in a proposed approach, and to address them prior to submitting the proposal. In addition, budgets should be scrutinized for precision and necessity in the calculation of each budgeted item.

BUSINESS EVALUATION

There are two areas of consideration encompassed by the business evaluation:

Areas of Analysis for the Business Evaluation

- Price and cost analysis
- Determination of contractor responsibility

Price and cost analysis is conducted as described in Chapter 6. Determination of contractor responsibility includes analysis of a potential contractor's financial strength and management capability. This includes the quality and appropriateness of organizational structure and design, past performance on similar efforts, reputation for reliability, availability of required facilities, cost controls, accounting policies and procedures, purchasing procedures, personnel practices, property accounting and control, and financial resources. All of these factors are evaluated in the context of the technical expertise needed as recommended by the technical evaluator(s).

Again it is important for prospective contractors who are hoping for a favorable evaluation to do whatever is possible to build credibility for its fiscal and management soundness, and that usually means periodic evaluation by outside experts. Recent reports by management experts who have positively evaluated management capability, by accountants who have audited fiscal records and found the agency fiscally sound, or program evaluators who have praised the quality of service can all help increase the likelihood of a positive business evaluation.

SELECTING POTENTIAL CONTRACTORS FOR NEGOTIATION

Data compiled from the technical and business evaluations form the basis for selection of proposals for negotiation and award of contracts. Neither technical superiority alone nor business superiority alone is grounds for selection. Likewise, weaknesses in either of these areas are not grounds for elimination. Once the technical and business evaluations are complete, they must be reconciled and proposals determined to be within the competitive range. Those prospective contractors determined to be within this range are then informed of those areas in which their proposals were evaluated as deficient and are given an opportunity to strengthen their proposals so that they may fully satisfy all requirements.

Coordinated effort between the contracting office and the program office is essential to ensure that all proposals within the competitive range are placed in contention for award of the contract. This coordinated effort is designed to "yield the true benefits of competition, in terms of better technical proposals, more realistic cost/price estimates, timely performance, and reduced negotiation effort" (USDHEW, 1971, p. 51).

Once all proposers who wish to continue the process have submitted their best and final proposals, selections are made for negotiation. Contract negotiation includes the following: (1) reaching agreement with a potential contractor on all of the requirements and provisions that will govern performance of the contract; (2) setting forth these terms in a mutually acceptable contractual document; and (3) justifying and documenting the contract negotiated (USDHEW, 1971).

In summary, the status of proposers changes as they proceed through each stage of the evaluation and negotiation process, as follows:

**Changing Statuses Throughout the Evaluation
and Negotiation Process**

From   Proposer or prospective contractor
To   Proposer in the competitive range

| To | Potential contractor |
| To | Contractor |

Proposers include all who respond to the RFP. Proposers in the competitive range include those who are not eliminated when the technical and business evaluations have been completed. Potential contractors are those selected for negotiations. Typically a government contracting agency will negotiate first with the potential contractor who offers the contract most advantageous to the government. If the contract cannot be negotiated with the first choice, the government will move on down the list until a successful contract is negotiated. Once a contract is awarded and signed, the potential contractor moves to the status of contractor.

THE CASE OF THE DETERMINED COMMUNITY

The State Department of Education initiated a major campaign to prevent and reduce drug use and abuse among high school youth. They planned to make $500,0000 available statewide for special projects to be proposed by local school districts, drug agencies, community groups, or other capable providers.

New Directions for Youth (NDY), a newly formed group of parents, school counselors, and professional drug counselors, submitted a comprehensive proposal for a relatively small school district that served only about 7500 students. The project was designed to provide intensive individual, group, and family counseling to hard-core drug users; to provide alternative, "positive identity" avenues for moderate drug users; and to provide retreats and mutual support groups focused on maintaining a positive identity and saying "no" to drugs for those who had never used them. Although the proposal was clearly superior to those received from other districts, there was a major problem: the cost was $50,000—10% of the total budget to serve less than 1% of the state's high school population.

The NDY Board was asked to cut the budget so that it more realistically reflected the district's share of the resources. Instead, they came back with a counteroffer. They said, "We believe so strongly in the merits of this program that we will do the following: (1) raise $10,000 ourselves from local sponsors, (2) ask the school district for in-kind contributions totaling $5,000, and (3) guarantee at least 500 volunteer hours per year from parents. In return we ask you to fund us at a level of $35,000 even though that is proportionally higher than our high school population would warrant." With such persuasive arguments and such a committed group of people behind the program, the Department could hardly refuse, and funded the program. It was a good decision. Ultimately the program became a model for districts of that type and size, and proved to be a most effective approach.

PREPARING FOR NEGOTIATIONS

Many authors on the subject of negotiation suggest that the beginning point for negotiations is a thorough knowledge of the content areas to be considered. In POSC this means that both government contracting agency and potential contractor negotiators have a complete knowledge of the RFP and the proposal. Negotiators should understand the spirit and intent of the RFP as well as the itemized requirements. It is also helpful to know something about previous experiences with service provision in this area of need. Who has provided services? How well or poorly? What programs have emerged over the years? What parts of this RFP are intended to address those problems?

Background information should be studied to prepare the government contracting agency and potential contractor negotiators to ask the appropriate questions and to have a frame of reference for understanding the answers. Past experience between government contracting agency and potential contractor is invaluable. It is also helpful to gather impressions about each agency's reputation in its community, its understanding of the problems and needs addressed by the RFP, its expertise in addressing them, and the possible risks and consequences of contracting with each potential contractor.

This knowledge of RFP and proposal leads to an identification of the specific technical and business content areas to be considered for negotiation. Each of these content areas, then, is subjected to a disciplined process, depicted in Figure 7.1. This process begins with identifying assumptions and ends with developing a negotiating position and reaching agreement on a decision (Nierenberg, 1973).

Assumptions are simple notions or ideas that are accepted for expediency's sake until they can be supported or discredited by data and information. In POSC it is seldom realistic to expect that every contingency will be covered in either the RFP or the proposal. Assumptions are an important part of the POSC process in human services, and they influence the negotiation process. They should, however, be clarified and substantiated before becoming a part of negotiations. In the foregoing case example, several assumptions are

Figure 7.1: Steps in the negotiating process.

evident. There is an assumption that hard-core drug users can be identified, that they and their families are willing to participate in counseling, and that counseling can be effective with this type of family. There is an assumption that moderate drug users need a more positive identity and that, if successful, this identity will lead to reduction or elimination of drug use. These are just a few examples of the types of assumptions that should be addressed in negotiation. Assumptions should not be allowed to be carried over into the contract. Wherever possible they should be clarified and substantiated, with factually based understandings made the basis of negotiations. The process of establishing facts may take place either prior to or during face-to-face negotiations.

Once understandings are established based on facts, issues can be developed. Nierenberg (1973) defines an issue as those factors on which one side takes an affirmative position and the other a negative position. Daley and Kettner (1981) define an issue as a point about which there is disagreement. If there is no disagreement, there is no issue. Technical issues and business issues should be itemized and written out because they will become the subjects of negotiation. For example, the intent of an RFP might be to reduce drug abuse among high school students through early intervention by (1) identifying at-risk students; (2) assigning a counselor; (3) conducting an assessment of the severity of the problem; and (4) placing the student in a mix of school and community programs based on assessed need. One of the proposals submitted is within the competitive range, but proposes to conduct an extensive, six- to eight-interview in-depth assessment of the student and his or her family situation prior to prescribing a service mix. Prenegotiation exploration reveals that the proposer is firm on this issue. The Department of Education's expectation is for a maximum of two assessment interviews prior to placement in a direct service program. This, then, becomes an issue for negotiation. Issues should be identified, itemized, and prioritized according to their importance or significance to the negotiator and their potential for affecting the success of this contract.

The next step is to take a position on an issue. The position taken does not typically represent a point. It is, more often, a range. Schatzki (1981) refers to this as the "settlement range," which he defines as the range of all possible settlements you would be willing to make in a given negotiation, from the very best to the very worst. The bottom end of the settlement range he calls the "least acceptable result" and the top the "maximum supportable position." The least acceptable result is that point in the range that separates a minimally acceptable contract from a contract that would be to a party's detriment. The maximum supportable position represents the most a party can ask for as an opening position without risking loss of credibility. Finding the extremes of the settlement range requires a good deal of knowledge, skill, experience, and work. Seldom in human services are there simple calculations or objective data that make any position clearly the "right" position. Each issue must be evaluated on its merits.

When the least acceptable result and maximum supportable position points are established, the settlement range becomes the focus of the negotiations. Rarely will either party to the negotiations voluntarily reveal its least acceptable result or its maximum supportable position. This is considered to be "giving away the store," and defeats the purpose of negotiation.

What is pursued in negotiation sessions is the overlap in settlement ranges, as illustrated in the following example. The executive director of a drug and alcohol detoxification center has served state clients for many years under a contract with the state. For three years there have been no increases in salaries to residential staff, and she is experiencing almost 100% turnover each year, low salaries having been identified as the cause. This time she goes in with a budget that includes an 18% raise for residential staff. The state, fearing precedent for other similar agencies, proposes 6%. As in all negotiations, neither position is firm. Each side has a settlement range. The executive director wants to find the state's least acceptable result (the highest percentage increase acceptable); the state probes to find the agency's least acceptable result (the lowest percentage increase acceptable). If the negotiations are to be successful, there must be overlap. If the state's range is 6% to 14%, and the agency's range is 10% to 18%, there is overlap, and successful negotiations can result. If, however, the state establishes a range of 6% to 10% and the agency 12% to 18%, the negotiations will fail to achieve a mutually satisfying figure. Figure 7.2 illustrates the overlap in settlement ranges.

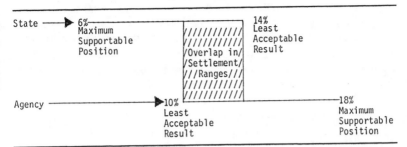

Figure 7.2: An illustration of overlap in settlement ranges.

The final step in negotiating is reaching agreement and making a decision that both parties will abide by that agreement. Nierenberg (1973) makes several important points about reaching agreement. Negotiation, he says, is not a game or a war—the objective is not a defeated or a dead opponent. This is especially relevent in POSC. Often the government contracting agency, exercising the full range of its funding and decision-making power, could impose its maximum supportable position in many instances. The price to be paid, however, will probably not be worth the "victory." Services to clients will most certainly suffer, and sometimes the quantity and quality of those services can be a matter of life and death. Morale among community agency staff will suffer as will relationships and trust between government contracting agency and contractors. Says Nierenberg, if you win every point, the negotiations may well have failed. On each issue it is important to go beyond a simple attempt to achieve one's maximum supportable position, and to determine "how much is this issue worth to us? What will a loss mean to them?" A successful negotiation, then, would reveal a mix of agreements ranging from achieving one's maximum supportable position on some issues to settling for one's least acceptable result on others.

STYLES OF NEGOTIATION

A number of authors on the subject of negotiation address the importance of style as a significant variable in determining the success of outcomes (Cohen, 1980; Levin, 1980; Schatzki, 1981; Warschaw, 1980). Clever names are often ascribed to characterize a style of negotiating. Warschaw (1980) labels six styles: jungle fighters, dictators, silhouettes, big daddies and big mamas, soothers, and win-win negotiators. Cohen characterizes two styles of negotiating: winning at all cost and negoti-

ating for mutual satisfaction. Filley, House, and Kerr (1976) concep-
tualize a continuum with a tough battler (one who wants to win at all
costs) at one extreme and a friendly helper (one who gives in at the first
sign of conflict) at the other. At the center of the continuum is the
problem solver, a person who looks for alternatives that will meet the
needs of both parties.

Three methods of negotiation have been described as win-lose, lose-
lose, and win-win (Filley, House, & Kerr, 1976). Win-lose tactics include
dominance through power, resisting influence, majority rule, and
railroading. Lose-lose methods include compromise, resort to arbitra-
tion, and resort to rules. Win-win methods include consensus building
(reaching a decision not unacceptable to anyone) and problem solving (a
search for creative alternatives). The authors draw an important
distinction between compromise, a lose-lose method, and problem
solving, a win-win method. Compromise they view as simply finding a
midpoint somewhere between the two positions and agreeing to settle on
that point. For example, if management offers a 4% wage increase and
labor is requesting 10%, compromise would dictate settling for something more than 4 and less than 10. Using compromise, both sides lose
something and neither is completely happy. Problem solving, on the
other hand, involves a search for creative alternatives. Applied to the
previous example, management might offer the full 10%, but propose
elimination of certain positions through attrition. Both sides get
something they want, and both can claim victory.

Services procured through POSC are usually highly complex,
involving many components. Although this can set the scene for long,
drawn out negotiations if there are many areas of disagreement, it can
also be an advantage. Given the components of program design and
service delivery, it is highly likely that there are creative alternatives—
win-win positions to be found—if only they are pursued diligently
enough.

SUMMARY

- The objective of negotiation in POSC is not "winning" but rather finding
  the best mutually acceptable solution.
- A proposal evaluation process will help determine which proposals are to
  be considered for negotiation.
- Selecting the best proposals involves both a technical and a business
  analysis and evaluation.
- Proposals for negotiation are selected from among those proposals
  considered to be in the competitive range.

- Negotiation involves a process of identifying assumptions, establishing facts, developing issues, taking a position, and negotiating a decision.
- The most productive approach to negotiation is usually the problem-solving or win-win approach.

EXERCISE

The Franklin County Department of Human Resources has been charged with the responsibility of serving the county's chronically mentally ill (CMI) population. They have chosen to do this through POSC with a request for proposals as the procurement methodology. Agencies that submitted proposals are agencies the county has had contracts with for years and provide drug, alcohol, and mental health services to the general population. New Beginnings is an agency that submitted a proposal that identifies the following services:

- Counseling to strengthen relationships with families and natural helping networks.
- Advice and counseling to ensure that clients secure optimum housing arrangements.
- Advice and counseling to ensure regular income through employment, welfare programs, or other options.
- Referral to appropriate sources to learn activities of daily living.

New Beginnings is a large agency. The county needs them if it is to have an impact on the CMI problem. But the proposal clearly leaves the impression that what is proposed is an in-office counseling program. What the county wants to provide is an aggressive outreach, case-finding, and "hands-on" helping program to get CMIs situated in adequate housing with a dependable income and support system. The issues to be negotiated are the following:

- housing
- income
- support system
- development of skills in activities of daily living

Develop a proposed settlement range for the County Human Resources Department on each of these issues.

Chapter 8

THE POSC CONTRACT

OBJECTIVES

By the end of this chapter the reader should be able to:

- Define the following key concepts:
  - General provisions
  - Special provisions
  - Cost reimbursement contracts
  - Unit cost contracts
  - Fixed-fee contracts
  - Incentive contracts
- Discuss or explain the following:
  - The order of precedence in a POSC contract
  - The relationship between POSC contract types and the partnership market continuum
- Perform the following functions:
  - Given a particular procurement, propose the appropriate POSC contract types that can be used

---

The purpose of work statement preparation, procurement, cost and price analysis, and contract negotiations is the awarding and signing of a POSC contract. It is in the best interest of both government contracting agency and contractor that the most accurate, precise, and complete document possible be developed for signatures. In this chapter, the preferred POSC contract format is presented, followed by a discussion of the various types of POSC contracts and their relationship to the partnership market continuum and to procurement.

THE CASE OF THE MISSING SPECIFICATIONS

A regional area agency on aging viewed contract preparation as essentially a legal matter and assigned responsibility for drafting each POSC contract to the agency's legal council. The attorney's preference was to utilize one unbroken document with many individual clauses rather than a contract divided into the sections of (1) cover sheet; (2) work statement; (3) special provisions; and (4) general provisions.

Emphasis in developing the document was placed on the details associated with liability, disputes, indemnity, and all other legal matters or contingencies that might arise and lead to a possible lawsuit. No work statement was included, and the precise definitions required for a clear mutual understanding of contract expectations were not written into the document.

A contract for home-delivered meals was awarded to a local restaurant. A section of the contract stated that the contractor was to provide home-delivered meals to 42 clients between the hours of 5:00 and 7:00 p.m. seven nights a week. Each day the contractor packaged what he could not sell—his leftovers—and had them delivered to clients in fulfillment of the contract. The area agency on aging was besieged with complaints from clients and their families and requested an in-person meeting with the contractor. When they met to discuss the problem of quality and quantity of food served, they discovered that the contractor was in full compliance with the terms of the contract.

Fortunately for the agency and the clients, the contractor agreed to the insertion of a work statement through a contract amendment. After this experience, the agency always used the standard POSC contract format to avoid leaving out an important part through oversight.

THE PREFERRED POSC CONTRACT FORMAT

POSC contracts take a variety of forms. Some are simple, one-page documents, others are complex lengthy documents. Length and complexity do not necessarily make a good POSC contract. Neither, however, does simplicity. It is doubtful whether a one-page contract can contain the necessary clauses needed to protect both the government contracting agency and the contractor.

There is a generally preferred POSC contract format used by the federal government, many states, and numerous county and municipal government contracting agencies. The format can be used as a point of departure for government contracting agencies developing their first POSC contracts or as a model by which government contracting agencies and contractors can evaluate their existing POSC contracts. The preferred POSC contract format consists of four parts:

The Parts of a POSC Contract

- Cover page
- Work statement
- General provisions
- Special provisions

COVER PAGE

The cover page is designed to communicate information about the POSC contract and to facilitate administrative processing. Figure 8.1 is an example of a POSC contract cover page. As the example illustrates, the cover page contains the important information about the POSC contract, its purpose, the parties involved, the contract term, and the amount of money involved. The cover page serves as a handy, one-page summary of the POSC contract. It can be used by the government contracting agency as an input document or data collection instrument for its POSC information system or by the contractor as a handy reference document. In addition, the cover page also groups together in one place all of the necessary contract signatures. Although seemingly a trivial matter, the cover page can save government contracting agencies and their staff attorneys a considerable amount of time considering the hundreds of POSC contracts that may be awarded in a year's time.

WORK STATEMENT

The work statement has already been discussed in Chapter 4. The necessity for, and importance of, the work statement to the final POSC contract document cannot be overstated. Attempts to translate a work statement into a simple or shorter document can create many more problems than they solve, as illustrated in the case example.

GENERAL PROVISIONS

The purpose of the general provisions is to group in one section all of the contractual terms and conditions that are common to all of a

CONTRACT FOR SERVICES
FREEPORT COUNTY DEPARTMENT OF SOCIAL SERVICES
2601 East Liberty Way, Fairview, XX 10001

1. Contract No.: _____   2. Contract Type: _____

2. Contract Amount: $_____   4. Purpose: _____

5. Fund Source: _____   6. **Contractor FEI/SSN** _____

7. Start Date: _____   8. Expiration Date: _____

This Contract is entered into by and between _____,
hereinafter referred to as Contractor, and Freeport County. The Contractor, for and in consideration of the covenants and conditions set forth herein, shall provide and perform the services as set forth below. All rights and obligations of the parties shall be governed by the terms of this document, its Exhibits, Attachments and Appendices, including any Subcontracts or Amendments as set forth herein and in:

This Contract contains all the terms and conditions agreed to by the parties. No other understanding, oral, or otherwise, regarding the subject matter of this Contract shall be deemed to exist or to bind any of the parties hereto. Nothing in this Contract shall be construed as a consent to any suit or waiver of any defense in a suit brought against the State of

_____ , Freeport County, or Contractor, in any State or Federal Court.

Notice under this Contract shall be given by personal delivery or by registered or certified mail to the addresses set forth below and shall be effective upon receipt by the party to whom addressed unless otherwise indicated in said notice.

Notice to Contractor: _____

Address: _____

Notice to Freeport County: Social Services Administration Contracts Coordinator

Address: _____ 2601 East Liberty Way, Fairview, XX 10001 _____

IN WITNESS WHEREOF, the parties enter into this Contract:

CONTRACTOR	FREEPORT COUNTY BOARD OF SUPERVISORS

By: _____   By: _____
      Signature/Title   Date   Chairman

RECOMMENDED BY: ATTEST:

_____   _____
Director   Date   Clerk of the Board   Date

This contract has been reviewed by the undersigned Deputy County Attorney who has determined that it is proper in form and is within the power and authority granted under the laws of the State of_____ .

_____   _____
Deputy County Attorney   Date

Figure 8.1: Example of a POSC Cover Page.

government contracting agency's POSC contracts regardless of the service or fund sources involved. The general provisions are sometimes referred to as the contract "boilerplate." Public attorneys are most concerned with and spend most of their time scrutinizing the general provisions in POSC contract because it is in this part that most general contract clauses appear. Contractors should have a clear understanding of the implications of each clause for the agency, and should secure legal advice if there are any areas of uncertainty. The general provisions of POSC contracts will usually contain clauses dealing with most, if not all, of the following areas:

General Provision Clauses

- Definitions
- Amendments
- Assignments
- Subcontracting
- Disputes
- Changes
- Termination
- Default
- Nonliability

- Indemnity
- Insurance/Bonding
- Nondiscrimination
- Equal employment opportunity
- Client grievance procedures
- Minimum wage
- Retention of records

The wording of specific general provision clauses is a technical and legal matter, and is beyond the scope of this chapter. The following sources, however, do provide suggestions about the wording of general provisions clauses and, in some cases, actual recommended wording: American Bar Association (1981), National Alliance of Business (n.d.), Franklin and White (1975), Federal Acquisition Regulations (Chapter 1, *Code of Federal Regulations*).

SPECIAL PROVISIONS

It often happens in POSC that general provisions (which apply to all of the government contracting agency's POSC contracts) are too general to cover certain items, and the work statement (which is specific to this contract only) is too specific to cover them. For this reason, special provisions are used to cover any special terms and conditions not covered by the work statement or the general provisions. For example, the special provisions can be used to do the following: (1) reference a particular set of cost principles or federal regulations, (2) set forth the compensation to be paid the contractor, (3) specify the method of payment or reimbursement, (4) set forth any special clauses required by the nature of the service involved, or (5) accomplish any other special purpose not generally applicable to all of the contracts.

The special provisions can also serve to override the general provisions. When some factor unique to an individual contract is not in harmony with a clause of the general provisions, two options are available to the government contracting agency: (1) the clause can be removed from the general provisions, or (2) a clause can be added to the special provisions overriding the clause of the general provisions and thus negating or altering it. In order to preclude having to change general provisions clauses constantly, many government contracting agencies prefer the approach of simply overriding the general provisions by the use of a special provisions clause.

The special provisions can be used to override the general provisions because there is an order of precedence to a POSC contract. Whenever there is an inconsistency between the special provisions and the general provisions, the special provisions control. Whenever there is an inconsistency between the work statement and the special or general provisions, the work statement controls. Underlying the order of precedence is a basic deductive logic that, as a POSC contract moves from the general to the specific, any inconsistencies should be resolved in favor of the specific. Because the work statement is the most specific part of a POSC contract, it controls in all cases. Because the special provisions are more specific than the general provisions, the special provisions control.

Order of Precedence in a POSC Contract

- Work statement
- Special provisions
- General provisions

In summary, there are three major reasons for use of a uniform POSC contract format:

Reasons for Using the Preferred POSC Contract Format

- Attorney familiarity
- Separation of legal and service considerations
- Preclusion of errors of omission

The preferred POSC contract format is essentially the standard government contract format. As such, public attorneys and private agency attorneys can become familiar with its construction and thus can review and process contracts for award quite rapidly.

By separating the work statement from other parts of the POSC contract, legal and service considerations are separated. Just as a social worker lacking formal legal training should not write general provision clauses, attorneys with no human services training should not write work statements. Separation of the legal and service areas helps to reduce interprofessional meddling.

And finally, by having special provisions, there is no need to alter the general provisions. Those aspects of an individual POSC contract unique to that contract can be dealt with in the special provisions. Most of the clauses designed to protect the interest of the government contracting agency and the contractor are contained in the general provisions. By not physically altering the general provisions from contract to contract, the potential for inadvertently omitting, deleting, or altering an important clause is reduced.

POSC CONTRACT TYPES

Government contracts are often categorized according to the method of contractor payment. One government contracting agency may be said to prefer "cost reimbursement" contracts; another may lean toward "unit cost" contracts. There are several different types of government contracts; four are most frequently used in POSC:

Contract Types Most Frequently Used in POSC

- Cost reimbursement
- Unit cost
- Fixed fee
- Incentive

COST REIMBURSEMENT

A cost reimbursement POSC contract is distinguished by the inclusion of a budget. The budget is a part of the contract and is used as a basis for paying the contractor for performance of contracted services. The use of the term "reimbursed" is important. For a cost to be reimbursed, it must first be incurred. This is important for two reasons.

First, the total budgeted figure for the contract may not be the same as the amount actually paid on the contract. If a cost item identified in the budget is not incurred by the contractor, it is not reimbursed. Second, it is important because of potential cash flow problems. A contractor under a cost reimbursement contract should be able to pay all expenses for at least 60 days while waiting for reimbursement. Cost reimbursement contracts are fairly common in POSC for human services.

UNIT COST

A unit cost POSC contract is one in which the contractor is paid by the unit. A unit cost is established in the contract, and the contractor simply bills the government contracting agency for the number of units provided. For example, a contractor providing home-delivered meals might be paid a price of $3 per meal delivered. If the contractor provided 1,000 meals during a month, he or she would bill the government contracting agency for $3,000. The use of the term "paid" rather than "reimbursed" is significant, because paid does not connote that a contractor actually incurred costs equal to the amount of compensation received. Under a unit cost contract, a contractor—even a nonprofit contractor—can earn a profit in one of two ways. First, there can be a cost savings incurred by the contractor that was not anticipated when the unit cost price was established. For example, the price of certain food commodities may have dropped due to a short-term oversupply. Second, the contractor can simply factor a profit margin into the price at which he or she offers to provide the service. If the government contracting agency accepts the offered price, it has also accepted the contractor's profit. Unit cost contracts are common in POSC in areas such as day-care and nursing care where a cost per day can be calculated.

FIXED-FEE

The fixed-fee POSC contract is characterized by the determining of a total price, which is payable upon completion of the service. A fixed-fee contract is often associated with the provision of a project-type service (i.e., a service that has a definable start and end point.) A fixed-fee POSC contract could be used, for example, in conducting a program evaluation. Upon provision of the required evaluation service and delivery of the final report, the contractor is paid the full fee or price.

INCENTIVE

An incentive POSC contract is a unit cost POSC contract with special incentives included. In an incentive contract, all or a portion of the contractor's compensation is tied to performance. For example, a training contractor might be paid 85% of its unit cost for graduating a client from its welding program and 15% of its unit cost when the client has worked in a nongovernment-subsidized job for a period of at least sixty days. Incentive contracts represent a method by which a contractor's compensation, and consequently its focus, can be redirected from the provision of services to the achievement of results.

POSC CONTRACT TYPES AND THE PARTNERSHIP/MARKET CONTINUUM

As Figure 8.2 illustrates, POSC contract types fall at different places along the partnership/market continuum. In a cost reimbursement contract, contractors are essentially held harmless as service providers by having all costs covered by the government contracting agency. This approach falls toward the extreme partnership end of the continuum. Conversely, unit-cost, fixed-fee, and incentive contracts are more characteristic of the market model. These contract types require that contractors assume responsibility for cost control and productivity because a predetermined price is paid for services regardless of actual costs. The incentive contract with its emphasis upon the achievement of results (i.e., outputs and/or outcomes) is considered to be closest to the market end of the continuum.

POSC CONTRACT TYPES AND PROCUREMENT

There is a relationship between the type of procurement used by a government contracting agency and the type of POSC contract that should ultimately result. Figure 8.3 illustrates this relationship. The major point to be made here is that the cost reimbursement contract is used only with competitive negotiation. Formal advertising and two-step formal advertising are designed to solicit unit cost or fixed-fee offers. The purpose of these two approaches is undermined when a contractor is awarded a cost reimbursement contract. As the POSC process becomes more refined over time, it is likely that more and more services will be contracted using unit cost, fixed-fee, and incentive contracts.

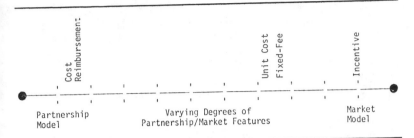

Figure 8.2: An illustration of where different POSC contract types fall on the partnership/market continuum.

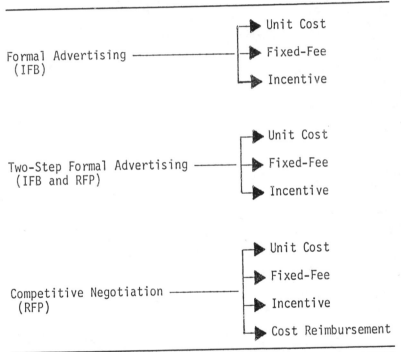

Figure 8.3: An illustration of the relationship between procurement types and POSC contract types.

SUMMARY

- The preferred POSC contract format has four parts: cover page, work statement, general provisions, and special provisions.

- The general provisions contain the contract clauses generally applicable to all of a government contracting agency's POSC contracts.
- The special provisions contain contract clauses relating to the contracted service, its funding source, or other special requirements specific to the contract.
- There are four major POSC contract types: cost reimbursement, unit cost, fixed-fee, and incentive.
- Cost reimbursement contracts are more characteristic of the partnership model of POSC, whereas unit cost, fixed-fee, and incentive contracts are more characteristic of the market model.

Part III

POSTAWARD ADMINISTRATION

Chapter 9

CONTRACT ADMINISTRATION

OBJECTIVES

By the end of this chapter the reader should be able to:

- Define the following terms:
  - contract administration
  - contract administrator
  - contract modification
  - "changes" clause
  - "disputes" clause
  - change order
  - patent ambiguity
  - specific performance
  - POSC monitoring
  - POSC information system
- Discuss or explain the following:
  - the major activities in contract administration
  - the purpose of POSC monitoring
  - the steps in building an information system for POSC

For the contractor a critical part of carrying out the contract successfully is a good working relationship with the contract administrator. Styles of contract administration can range from an "enforcer" at one extreme to a total "hands off" approach at the other. Neither extreme is in the best interest of the contractor. Ideally, a contract administrator will be in total harmony with the contractor in terms of commitment to provide the best possible services to clients within the limitations established by the contract. This focus can help avoid a "we-they" mentality and can provide a positive context for creative problem solving.

In the broadest sense, the term "contract administration" in POSC for human services can be defined as all those activities, on the part of the government contracting agency, that take place during contract performance.

Definition of Contract Administration

All those activities, on the part of the government contracting agency, that take place during performance of the contract. (General Service Administration, n.d.)

The performance period of a contract can be thought of as starting when the contract is signed and continuing until the contract is executory, that is, until all parties have discharged all of their contractual obligations. Contract administration activities are conducted for and on behalf of the government contracting agency by a person designated as a "contract administrator." In this chapter the role of the contract administrator is discussed and the major activities of contract administration identified.

THE CASE OF THE ORAL MONITORING REPORT

New Careers for the Disabled (NCD) was a sheltered workshop that provided on-the-job training for physically handicapped and developmentally disabled clients. For many years they operated on donations, United Way funds, client fees, and grants. Now the State Department of Social Services (DSS) wanted to purchase 240 slots per year for its physically and developmentally disabled clients.

There was little difficulty in developing, negotiating, and signing the contract. The Department of Social Services knew exactly what it wanted to purchase, and New Careers for the Disabled submitted a proposal that was responsive to all requirements of the RFP.

When a contract administrator came to monitor the contract at the end of the third month, she found incomplete records and no documentation of services provided or results achieved. The NCD director had arranged instead for a conference with each of the shop foremen who proceeded to describe progress and results with state clients served to date. When told that this procedure was not in compliance with the contract, the NCD director explained that this is how they had always functioned, that they have been highly successful, and that they had no intention of changing. The contract administrator said she had no choice and would withhold reimbursement until the necessary documentation was completed.

THE ROLE OF THE CONTRACT ADMINISTRATOR

Regardless of the name or job title (e.g., project manager, service specialist, field specialist, or some other name), any individual with delegated authority to represent the government contracting agency in contract administration dealings with the contractor is acting as a "contract administrator."

The contract administrator is the liaison between the government contracting agency and the contractor and, as such, has an interest in successful and productive contractor performance. The role of the contract administrator is to protect the interests of the government contracting agency by ensuring that the contractor performs in a satisfactory manner, while not infringing on the contractor's right to make its own management decisions (*Government Contract Administration,* General Services Administration, n.d.).

The role of the contractor is to protect the interests of agency, staff, and clients by ensuring contract compliance and proper documentation. This is usually accomplished best by careful attention by the agency administrator to services delivered under the contract, to record keeping, billing, reporting, making time available to the contract administrator, and generally being as cooperative as time constraints and agency pressures will allow. Problems should be addressed with the contract administrator in as open and forthright a manner as circumstances will permit.

A contract administrator should possess formal delegated authority to represent the government contracting agency. Put another way, the contract administrator should be the agent of the government contracting agency. A problem that occurs all too frequently in POSC for human services at the state and local government levels, but not at the federal level, is that contract administrators are not formally designated.

In the absence of a formal (i.e., written), designation a contractor is placed in the untenable position of having to rely on the instructions and contract interpretations of an individual whose authority to represent the government contracting agency is not verifiable. To preclude such situations, the contract administrator should either be named in the contract document itself or identified in a cover letter. This procedure affords the contractor some measure of legal protection in exchange for reliance on the instructions of the contract administrator. The formal designation of the contract administrator is a necessary preparatory step in contract administration.

THE MAJOR ACTIVITIES OF CONTRACT ADMINISTRATION

Contract administration begins with a session on orientation to POSC policies and procedures and ends with completion and follow up activities. In between the beginning and the end, a range of activities and responsibilities of contract administration include the following:

Major Activities in Contract Administration

- Orienting the contractor
- Processing claims
- Modifying the contract
- Resolving disputes
- Interpreting the contract
- Contract monitoring

ORIENTING THE CONTRACTOR

Shortly after contract award and prior to commencement of service delivery, the government contracting agency usually conducts an orientation for its contractors—especially new contractors. The purposes of the contractor orientation are to (1) review the POSC contract, paying particular attention to the work statement and those contract clauses that may be unfamiliar to new contractors; (2) explain billing and reporting requirements; and (3) provide the contractor with a copy of the monitoring instrument, if available. Providing a contractor with this information prior to service implementation sets an important tone for the working relationship between government contracting agency and contractor. Explaining key clauses, billing and payment/reimbursement procedures, and monitoring practices will help establish a relationship based on openness and trust. This type of relationship can pay significant dividends if problems arise during the life of the contract.

PROCESSING CLAIMS

Processing contractor claims for payment or reimbursement is a fairly routine activity. Claims are verified and processed as quickly as possible to ensure uninterrupted cash flow to the contractor. A contract administrator should never use the claims processing activity as a method of punishing a problem contractor. Processing claims is simply a business transaction between two parties. If it is used for any purpose other than this, the credibility of the contract administrator will be seriously damaged in all interactions, not just those related to billing and processing claims.

Instances may arise, however, when a contract administrator may have to withhold a contractor's payment or reimbursement to force compliance with the contract. Although somewhat of an extraordinary action, withholding funds may be the only avenue open to a contract administrator—short of terminating the contract—to gain a contractor's attention. Even when this drastic action is necessary, however, it is important that transactions are conducted in a businesslike manner, with complete documentation backing up the decision and with the contractor fully informed.

MODIFYING THE CONTRACT

Seldom, if ever, will every possible contingency and problem related to a contract be anticipated in advance by the government contracting agency. Thus it is usually necessary to modify a contract at least once during its term. POSC contract modifications can take two forms:

Forms of POSC Modifications

- Contract amendment
- Change order

A contract amendment is essentially a new contract, the terms of which modify an existing contract. Because it is a new contract, a contract amendment is a bilateral action requiring the agreement of both the government contracting agency and the contractor. Contract amendments can be used to alter the work statement or any clauses of the general provisions or special provisions.

A change order is a unilateral action on the part of the government contracting agency. A change order is a formal written order altering some part of the work statement—frequently some design specification that is not working as anticipated. Figure 9.1 is an example of a change order.

The authority for a government contracting agency to issue a change order unilaterally comes from the inclusion of a "changes" clause in the contract, usually as part of the general provisions. When a contractor signs a POSC contract that includes a "changes" clause, the contractor is essentially agreeing to allow the government contracting agency to make unilateral alterations in the work statement. If the POSC contract does not contain a "changes" clause, the only method of contract modification is the contract amendment. The following example of a "changes" clause for use in POSC is based on a "changes" clause used by the federal government.

An Example of a POSC Changes Clause

The contract administrator may at any time, by written order, make changes within the general scope of the contract in the work statement. If any such change causes an increase or decrease in the compensation to be paid or reimbursed to the contractor, an equitable adjustment shall be made. Any claim by the contractor for an adjustment under this clause must be asserted within 30 days from the date of receipt by the contractor of the notification of change. Failure to agree to any adjustment shall constitute a dispute within the meaning of the clause of this contract entitled "disputes." However, nothing in this clause shall excuse the contractor from proceeding with the contract as changed.

A "changes" clause means exactly what it says. The contract administrator may make changes at any time and the contractor must implement the changes even if he or she disagrees. In the event of a disagreement or dispute, the "disputes" clause of the contract provides a mechanism for the contractor to seek redress.

RESOLVING DISPUTES

What happens when a dispute arises between the government contracting agency and the contractor? If the POSC contract contains a disputes clause, an administrative mechanism is invoked. The following is an example of a "disputes" clause that has been used in POSC contracts by the State of Arizona.

CONTRACT NO. _____   CHANGE NO. _____

CHANGE ORDER TO THE CONTRACT FOR SERVICES
BETWEEN
THE SEASIDE COUNTY DEPARTMENT OF HUMAN SERVICES
AND

I.   Pursuant to the authority stated in Clause 21, *Changes* of the General
     Provisions of the Contract, the following Contract change(s) are here-
     by ordered (add attachments if necessary):

II. The effective date of this Contract Change is _____ .

III. The foregoing paragraphs contain all the changes made by this change
     order. All other terms and conditions of the original contract and
     previous modifications remain in full force and effect.

IN WITNESS WHEREOF, the parties acknowledge and agree upon this
change:

CONTRACTOR   SEASIDE COUNTY

_____   _____
Authorized Signature   Contract Administrator

_____   _____
Date   Date

The Contractor is directed to sign three (3) copies, retain one copy and
return two (2) copies to the Contract Administrator.

Figure 9.1: An Example of a Change Order.

Example of a Disputes Clause

Except as otherwise provided for in this contract, any dispute concerning a question of fact arising under this contract that is not disposed of by agreement between the parties within a reasonable time shall be decided by the contract administrator who shall reduce his or her decision to writing and mail, or otherwise furnish a copy thereof, to the contractor. The decision of the contract administrator shall be final and conclusive unless, within thirty (30) calendar days from the date of mailing of such copy, the director receives a written request for appeal of the contract administrator's decision. Pending a final decision of a dispute hereunder, the contractor shall proceed diligently with the performance of the contract administrator's decision.

Clearly the message in the "changes" and "disputes" clauses is that differences should be resolved between the contract administrator and contractor. Problems should be elevated to the level of the director only as a last resort. It is the responsibility of the contract administrator to attempt to resolve disputes to the mutual satisfaction of all parties so that services are not disrupted and clients continue to be served. POSC contracts that do not include a "disputes" clause run the risk that a dispute may disrupt services, be harmful to clients, and may ultimately have to be resolved in court.

INTERPRETING THE POSC CONTRACT

Another of the major activities of contract administration is interpreting the POSC contract. It is the contract administrator who is the official interpreter of the contract terms and conditions. In the following section some of the more common rules of contract interpretation are set forth.

The contractor's objective interpretation. A basic rule of government contract law is that where there is a reasonable alternative interpretation of a contract provision, the words will be construed against the party that drafted them. If a work statement provision or a contract clause is ambiguous and the contractor relied upon a reasonable alternative interpretation, the courts will generally rule on behalf of the contractor. It is not what the government contracting agency meant to say that counts, but what was actually said. The general rule does not apply to situations in which a patent ambiguity is held to exist.

Patent Ambiguity. If a work statement provision or a contract clause is so obviously incorrect or inconsistent that the contractor should know something is wrong, a patent ambiguity is deemed to exist. For example, if a contractor's copy of a contract did not contain a work statement although the work statement was referenced elsewhere in the contract, the contractor is expected to recognize that a patent ambiguity exists. When a contractor encounters a patent ambiguity, he or she has a responsibility to contact the contract administrator and request a clarification. Once a clarification has been provided, the contractor cannot disavow the clarification, although he or she can disagree with the interpretation and invoke the "disputes" clause.

Contract read as a whole. A government contract constitutes a whole, and no single part can be interpreted in isolation from the others. It is this principle that provides for the order of precedence in government contracts. A work statement supercedes special provisions, and a special provision clause supercedes a general provision clause. If a contract stipulates one requirement in the general provisions and a contradictory requirement in the work statement, the language of the work statement governs because the contract is interpreted as a whole and complete document, not as a series of unrelated clauses.

Incorporation by reference. Many POSC contracts include references to other documents. The referenced documents can range from federal laws and regulations to state statutes, to local government ordinances, and to a variety of other documents. As a general rule, a document incorporated in a POSC contract by reference is just as much a part of the contract as if the referenced document was physically attached to the contract. Contractors should understand this principle and should get copies of, read, and comply with the requirements of all documents included by reference in their POSC contracts.

Specific performance. In all government contracts, the government contracting agency is entitled to specific performance with the design specifications of the work statement; that is, when the government contracting agency uses design specifications, the contractor must comply with them to the letter. If this poses problems in POSC, they can be addressed through the "changes" and "disputes" clauses, but contractors are expected to provide the service in accordance with all requirements included in design specifications or run the risk of being out of compliance with the terms of the contract.

CONTRACT MONITORING

POSC monitoring can be defined as follows:

Definition of POSC Monitoring

- the periodic review and
- documentation of
- the contractor's progress in fulfilling the stated terms and conditions of the contract,
- the identification of areas requiring corrective action, and
- follow-up to ensure that corrective action is successfully taken

---

"Periodic review" suggests a frequency of more than once a year. Frequency will depend on the nature of the contract and previous experience with the contractor. "Documentation" suggests the ability to support, with objective evidence, the monitoring observations made and conclusions drawn. "Progress in fulfilling the stated terms and conditions of the contract" suggests that the contract itself, with its stated terms and conditions, is the source of criteria by which contractor performance is monitored. "The identification of areas requiring corrective action" indicates that monitoring is not a static but a dynamic function that identifies problems or issues that need to be addressed either during this contract period or prior to the next one. And finally, "follow-up to ensure that corrective action is successfully taken" suggests that internal mechanisms are in place within the government contracting agency to deal with problems once they are identified.

FACTORS AFFECTING THE QUALITY OF POSC MONITORING

Clearly contract monitoring is the most important single function of postaward administration. For this reason, we will cover monitoring in greater depth than other contract administration activities. In spite of the tremendous importance of this function, however, there is much evidence to suggest that contract monitoring is one of the most neglected and perhaps misunderstood functions in the POSC system. Several studies have revealed that little or no monitoring is done once a contract is implemented (Ghere, 1981; Pacific Consultants, 1979). Furthermore, lack of effective monitoring has been linked directly to problems in contract implementation (Comptroller General, 1980).

PURPOSE OF POSC MONITORING

POSC monitoring is not simply a matter of "checking up on the contractor." An effective monitoring system is directed to the achievement of a number of purposes (see Franklin & White, 1975).

Four Purposes of POSC Monitoring

- Assuring a sound and accountable POSC system
- Assuring contract compliance
- Problem identification
- Providing information for future planning

Assuring accountability refers to the responsibility of the POSC system to achieve the highest levels of effectiveness, efficiency, and relevance possible. Developing an accountable system depends on a number of factors. First, and probably most important, is the POSC philosophy of the government contracting agency. If the philosophy is to treat contracts as grants, then developing an accountable POSC system is problematic. Accountability begins with a clear philosophical position on relative roles and responsibilities of government contracting agency and contractor.

A second factor affecting accountability is the number of available contractors. If only one contractor exists or is willing and able to provide a particular service, the government contracting agency will have fewer options than when there are many contractors. If the one contractor persistently fails or refuses to comply with requests for accountable practices, the government contracting agency has only a few options (1) continue to collaborate in hopes of changing and improving their practices, (2) deliver services directly, (3) attempt to develop other prospective contractors.

A second purpose of POSC monitoring is to ensure contractor compliance with stated terms and conditions of the contract. Some documentation must be kept that will verify that the contractor is adhering to all work statement requirements as well as to the special and general provisions of the POSC contract. To do otherwise is to be in a state of contract noncompliance, which could lead to disallowed payments, audit exceptions, and the most severe of all actions—contract termination. Several factors can affect contract compliance.

One of the most difficult situations to deal with in contract monitoring is the discovery that the contractor simply is not capable of delivering the services promised in the contract. It is in hopes of avoiding this situation that the practice of establishing contractor responsibility (assuring that the contractor has the necessary staff and financial resources prior to contract award) was developed. When it becomes clear that contract compliance is not feasible, a contract administrator should either alter the contract requirements through a change order or amendment, or terminate the contract.

Ease of modification is another factor affecting compliance. Because it is difficult in human services to anticipate every contingency that may arise in the delivery of a contracted service, many government contracting agencies have developed POSC systems that allow for contract modification with relative ease, either through a formal contract amendment or by the initiation of a change order. Where contract modification has been made difficult, time consuming, and complex, contract monitors may find themselves in an awkward situation, either having to ignore an area of noncompliance or having to terminate an otherwise acceptable contract. Neither of these options is desirable.

Size of work load for contract administrators is yet another factor that can affect contract compliance. A variety of factors must be taken into consideration in calculating work load, including size and complexity of contracts, travel time, experience of the contractors, and others. Enough time should be available to become thoroughly familiar with the contracts, for adequate orientation of contractors, for multiple visits during the year, and for follow-up to correct problems identified.

The third purpose of monitoring is to identify problem areas. Problems identified may be limited to specific contracts, or they may be of a more general nature, cutting across many contracts. Problems of a recurring nature or those that affect many contracts usually indicate that the fault lies somewhere in the POSC system, and not necessarily with the contractor. Several factors affect problem identification.

One important factor is the timing and frequency of POSC monitoring visits. Timing can make a big difference in the successful identification and resolution of contracting problems. A visit that is scheduled too early into the contracting cycle may be completed before problems have had an opportunity to emerge. A visit that is scheduled too late into the cycle may allow problems to develop to the point where they can no longer be resolved. Appropriate timing of site visits often depends on the length of experience with a contractor. A new contractor should usually be targeted for an on-site POSC monitoring visit some time shortly after completion of the second or third month of service. This time frame permits the POSC monitor to review performance and compliance with the contractor with several monthly billings as a frame of reference, while identifying problems early enough so that they can be addressed early in the contracting cycle. Follow-up POSC monitoring visits for new contractors or those where problems have been identified should be made at least every ninety days. More experienced contractors with no problems identified in the initial POSC monitoring visit can be revisited less frequently.

Another source of information is the monthly reports and billings submitted by the contractor. These can often be studied and analyzed to detect problems that might interfere with satisfactory completion of the contract. Simple devices such as comparing one month's actual volume of service and expenditures to 1/12 of anticipated service volume and expenditures on a 12-month contract can reveal whether the volume of service being delivered and funds being spent are significantly ahead of or behind schedule. Under- or over-reporting or billing of service units is usually indicative that some problems are being experienced, and can, along with other indicators, be used as an early warning device.

Contractor-contract administrator relationships can also affect compliance. Contractors typically know when and where they are experiencing problems with contract compliance or service delivery. The question is whether or not they have the type of relationship with their contract administrator that will permit them to discuss problems openly. There is a natural fear of loss of funding, and they may be inclined to withhold information, depending on their perceptions of the monitor and the monitoring function. Simply stated, if they view POSC monitoring as a policing function, they will be less likely to discuss problems openly. If they view it as a consultative relationship, they will be more likely to share the details.

The fourth purpose of POSC monitoring is to collect information for planning. Ideally, data and information on both problems and strengths of the system can be used to strengthen and support the POSC planning system. In an effective planning system, reports and other available information will be disseminated throughout the organization so that new knowledge can be incorporated into the next round of planning. Several factors can affect a POSC system's capability to generate information useful for planning purposes.

First, a planning system will benefit from concise POSC monitoring reports that focus on problems and solutions. Much like case recording, POSC monitoring reports can take on the format of long, detailed narrative reports, or they can be designed to identify problem areas, summarize data that support existence of the problem, and pose alternative solutions. Long narrative reports are unlikely to initiate action, whereas problem-focused reports may lead to meaningful change.

Another factor affecting the planning function is the manner in which monitoring information is used by the government contracting agency. Recurring problems should not be left unattended. They require a careful analysis to determine why they continue to occur. An effective POSC monitoring system will be designed in a way that will ensure that such problems are addressed. Staff meetings, committees, task forces, and special assignments can be used to study problem areas and propose solutions.

DESIGNING A MANAGEMENT
INFORMATION SYSTEM FOR POSC

The effectiveness of monitoring and evaluation in POSC will depend to a large extent on the quality of data collected and the ways in which data are compiled and displayed for use in decision making. Maximizing the use of data and information on contract performance can often reduce the need for extensive time-consuming site visits and permit more precise focus on problems. Let us assume, for the moment, that four agencies had contracts to provide job-finding services for teenagers, and compilation of the first six months of reports revealed the profile shown in Table 9.1.

A simple table like this can be very revealing when it comes to POSC monitoring. Obviously the table will take on meaning only in relation to the contract, but a cursory examination indicates that Agencies A and D are probably proceeding satisfactorily in relation to meeting the terms of their contracts (that is, at the halfway point for the contract, they have served at least half the clients they contracted to serve). Agencies B and C, however, appear to be in trouble; Agency C in serious trouble. A data display such as Table 9.1 can direct activity toward helping those contractors in need of help while reducing time spent on contracts that appear to be proceeding without difficulty.

STEPS IN BUILDING AN
INFORMATION SYSTEM FOR POSC

Ever since the infusion of computerization into the processing of data in human services, organizations have seemingly experienced difficulty

TABLE 9.1
Example of an Output Table

	Agency A	Agency B	Agency C	Agency D	Totals
Number of clients contracted to serve	90	36	50	64	240
Number served to date	50	12	8	32	102
Number of job slots identified to date	84	30	12	72	198
Number of clients interviewed for jobs	46	8	1	30	85
Number hired	35	8	0	28	71
Number remaining 3 months or longer	16	8	0	25	49

in designing precise, streamlined, useful, and relevant information systems. Reams of printouts stacked on top of one another collecting dust are testimony to the problems of designing useful systems. The major problem is clearly that of overkill on data collection and processing. Much information is collected because it is "nice to know" and may be needed some day. Useful POSC monitoring systems, however, must resist that temptation and collect only what will be used, lest the whole system be rendered ineffective.

Step 1. Create an output table. One way to help ensure the collection and processing of useful data and information is to begin the design and development of the system by determining what information will be needed for monitoring and evaluation purposes. The answers will be found in the contract. Returning to prejob guidance and job placement as an example, let us assume that a contract contained the following specifications:

- To provide prejob counseling to at least _____ clients
- To screen clients for job aptitude and interest
- To find at least 3 job slots for each client and arrange interviews
- To match at least 75% of clients to jobs successfully
- To ensure that the ethnicity of clients served reflects the ethnicity of unemployed teenagers in the service area.

The first step in organizing the POSC data collection system is to create tables that display data in a way that pertinent questions can be answered about each of the specifications. The important point here is that then tables be created first, prior to the development of data collection instruments. A table designed to monitor the foregoing five specifications would use one or more rows for each specification, as follows:

- Number of clients in program to date
- Number screened for
  - aptitude
  - interest
- Number of clients who have interviewed for
  - 1 job
  - 2 jobs
  - 3 jobs
- Number of clients employed
- Ethnicity of clients
  - Asian
  - Black
  - Hispanic
  - Native American
  - White
  - Other

Once useful "dummy" tables have been created—tables that will answer important monitoring questions—system development proceeds to Step 2.

Step 2. Create input documents. An input document is just another name for a data collection instrument or, in this case, a monitoring instrument. There are two types of monitoring in POSC: desk monitoring and on-site monitoring. Desk monitoring consists of a review of all monthly reports and billings submitted by the contractor. Typically quantitative (numerical) data are extracted from these reports to complete the type of table illustrated in Table 9.1. These reports and billings are usually mailed in, and do not require a site visit.

On-site POSC monitoring is for the purpose of verifying that what is being reported and billed is actually being delivered and is in compliance with the terms and conditions of the contract. The key to successful on-site POSC monitoring lies in two simple principles: (1) monitoring is keyed to the contract. Nothing is monitored, no question is asked, no documentation is sought unless it relates to contract compliance. (It is important to remember here that evaluation data may also be collected at this time, but cannot be used for the monitoring of contract compliance.) (2) every issue of contract compliance is operationalized in a straightforward, objective manner, not subject to varying interpretations. This means that objective indicators of contract compliance must be developed. Wherever possible these indicators should rely on simple tests of accomplishment.

Using the prejob guidance and placement example, a monitoring instrument like the following might be constructed:

Example of a Monitoring Instrument

(1) Number of clients in program to date . . . . _____

    (a) there is a case record on each client   Yes   No

    (b) a random check showed records have
         all required forms completed   Yes   No

(2) Number of clients screened for aptitude . . . . _____

                       interest . . . . _____

    (a) Each client receives an aptitute test
         as verified in random check of records   Yes   No

    (b) Each client receives an interest test
         as verified in random check of records   Yes   No

(3) And so on.

An objective monitoring instrument, keyed to the contract, itemizing all issues of compliance, and stated as simple tests of accomplishment, can serve as a valuable tool in POSC monitoring. Any "no" answers to the foregoing questions would serve as a red flag, an early warning system that problems could exist or be developing in that area.

Step 3. Develop a data and information processing system. Data generated through monthly reports and billings will most likely be entered into a computer so that output tables can be produced. Timely entry and retrieval of data is important if the early warning concept is to be of value.

Data collected in on-site POSC monitoring takes the form of a report to the appropriate administrator in the government contracting agency. These reports are usually quite brief on a monthly basis, but are expanded on a quarterly or semiannual basis. Effective reports will highlight problem areas and make recommendations for problem resolution.

EVALUATION

Evaluation is a function that is separate and distinct from monitoring in POSC. Evaluation focuses on a range of efficiency, effectiveness, impact, and relevance questions that may go far beyond the limits of a contract.

For example, five different contractors may have contracts to provide congregate meals for the elderly. The contracts require that they serve nutritious, hot meals five times per week to every eligible participant. Monitoring systems would be designed to determine whether or not each contractor was following these specifications. Evaluation, however, may examine much broader questions. What effects do these meals have on the nutrition and health of the participants? Which of the five providers serves the most nutritious meal for the least money? What socialization benefits, if any, are derived from serving congregate meals as opposed to home-delivered meals?

In the process of exploring evaluation questions, it is entirely possible to discover that the program, as conceptualized and funded, was a total failure, yet every contractor was in full compliance with the contract. Evaluation is an extremely important function to determine how well clients are being served and what is accomplished through the POSC system. Program evaluation knowledge and skill requires a much more thorough coverage than is possible here. (For a comprehensive treatment of the subject of program evaluation in human services, see Austin, 1982.)

Clearly, from the foregoing discussion, the role of the contract administrator is an important one. Carrying out these responsibilities skillfully requires a thorough knowledge of POSC, the contract, and the services provided. The skills of diplomacy, tact, and cooperation are important to an overall, positive approach to contract administration, but ability to handle confrontation and conflict may also be necessary at times. A guiding principle for the contract administrator is that the primary purpose of the contract is always to provide the best possible services to clients and consumers. The contract administrator, therefore, serves as an advocate and representative for clients, always remembering that they are best served when the highest level of contract performance is achieved. Enabling and helping contractors to achieve this level of performance is the mark of a highly skilled and competent contract administrator.

SUMMARY

- Regardless of the name or job title, any person with formal delegated authority to represent the government contracting agency in dealings with a contractor is acting as a contract administrator.
- The major activities in contract administration include the following:
  - orienting the contractor
  - processing claims
  - modifying the contract
  - resolving disputes
  - interpreting the contract
  - monitoring the contract
- There are two methods by which a POSC contract can be modified: by a contract amendment or by issuance of a change order.
- Disputes are resolved between the contract administrator and contractor unless appealed to a higher level.
- The contract administrator is the official interpreter of contract terms and conditions, and complies with accepted rules of interpretation, including the following:
  - the contractor's objective interpretation
  - patent ambiguity
  - contract read as a whole
  - incorporation by reference
  - specific performance
- Contract monitoring is an important function in POSC that is designed to ensure contract compliance and act as an early warning system when problems emerge.
- Four purposes of POSC monitoring are as follows: assuring a sound and accountable system, contract compliance, problem identification, and planning.
- An information system for POSC should be designed so that both monitoring data and evaluation data can be collected in reports and site visits, but each set of data can be extracted for its separate and unique purpose.
- Effective POSC monitoring requires objective monitoring instruments that are keyed to the contract.

EXERCISE

Study the work statement in Appendix A and perform the following functions:

(1) Design a monitoring instrument to be used in monitoring contract compliance with design specifications, including the following:

- meal temperature
- nutritional information
- assessment of client need
- client contribution
- service tasks

(2) Design 3 output tables (one each for items, A, B, and C) that can be used to monitor Section VII Contract Objectives. Assume there are 3 contractors: Hot Meals for the Elderly (HME); Meals for the Needy (MFN); and Meals Express (MXP). Use these column headings. Remember to include enough data by the way you create your row headings that it will be possible to determine your basis for concluding whether or not the contractors are ahead of, behind, or on schedule.

Appendix A
Sample Work Statement

I. Service Definition

  This service provides a nutritious meal, containing at least one-third of the Recommended Dietary Allowance (RDA) for an individual, delivered to the client's own residence.

II. Definition of Terms

  Client means person sixty years of age or older who is a resident of Brookside County and has been determined to be eligible for county services. The legal spouse of any client is also eligible for home-delivered meals, regardless of age.

  Contractor means the person, firm, or organization performing the work described in this work statement.

  Contract Administrator means the person administering this contract on behalf of the Department.

  Department means the Brookside County Human Resources Department.

III. Enumeration of Standards

  (A) All meals prepared must contain at least one-third of the Recommended Dietary Allowance for an individual.

  (B) All facilities that prepare home-delivered meals must meet sanitation codes and regulations of the Brookside County Health Department.

  (C) All drivers must possess a valid driver's license.

IV. Design Specifications

  (A) Client, Staff, Materials, Facilities, or Equipment Requirements

    (1) Contractor shall make provision for keeping meals at 110 degrees F. during delivery.

    (2) Contractor shall ensure the development of, and submit to the Department for review, written menus that meet nutritional requirements.

    (3) Contractor shall develop and submit to the Department a written policy statement specifying the criteria to be used in assessing and periodically reassessing a client's need for home-delivered meals.

(4) Contractor shall establish a procedure to afford clients the opportunity to contribute toward part or all of the cost of the provision of services under this contract, including the following:

    (a) Each client shall determine in his or her own discretion the amount of any contribution.

    (b) The contractor's contribution procedure shall ensure the confidentiality of each contribution and that no distinction shall be made between clients who make contributions and those who do not or between clients based on size of contribution.

    (c) The contractor shall not require that clients make a contribution as a condition of service delivery.

    (d) The contractor shall maintain financial books and records sufficient to document the appropriate disbursement of all contributions.

(B) Service Tasks

    (1) Prepare a schedule for each client that includes the date and time the meal will be delivered.

    (2) Provide each client a copy of the menu at least one week in advance.

    (3) Prepare meals and arrange for the delivery of meals.

    (4) Deliver meal to the client at his or her place of residence.

    (5) Obtain client's signature and date for each meal delivered and maintain the signatures in the central file.

    (6) Measure the temperature of the last home-delivered meal served at least once a week.

V. Performance Specifications

(A) Output Definition

One client, having received and signed for at least 90% of the meals provided from the point of assessment to the point of reassessment shall be considered a service completion. Anyone receiving less than 90% of the meals provided shall be considered a dropout for monitoring and evaluation purposes. Output shall be determined from contractor's records, with random verifications to be conducted under the direction of the contract administrator.

(B) Outcome Definition

Change on the 5-point Brookside County Nutritional Measurement Scale, which ranges from "Severely malnourished" to "No symptoms of dietary deficiency," shall be used as a basis for monitoring and evaluating outcomes for this contract. Random measurements shall be conducted by nutritional specialists employed by the Department.

VI. Units of Service

(A) Material Unit: One meal per day per client shall equal one unit of service.

(B) Output Unit: One client having received and signed for at least 90% of meals provided from the point of assessment to the point of reassessment shall equal one output unit.

(C) Outcome Unit: Movement of one point on the 5-point Brookside County Measurement Scale shall equal one outcome unit.

VII. Contract Objectives

Satisfactory performance on this contract shall constitue the following:

(A) A minimum of 2600 home-delivered meals prepared and delivered in accordance with the requirements of this work statement prior to the expiration of this contract.

(B) At least an 80% service completion or output rate.

(C) At least 25% of output units will demonstrate a change of at least one outcome unit in a positive direction.

VIII. Administrative and Reporting Requirements

(A) The contractor shall maintain on file an updated "Participant Information Card" on all clients.

(B) The following reports shall be submitted by the contractor to the contract administrator in accordance with the specified time frames:

   (1) A correctly completed "Monthly Report of New Clients" by the close of the third working day of each month.

   (2) The correctly completed "Client Signature Sheets" by the close of the third working day of each month.

   (3) A correctly completed "Monthly Meals Summary Report" by the close of the third working day of each month.

   (4) A correctly completed "Menu Change Form" within five (5) working days of any change.

   (5) A correctly completed "Project Income Report" by the close of the third working day of each month.

Appendix B
Sample Request for Proposals

REQUEST FOR PROPOSALS
FOR
HOMEMAKER SERVICES

June 23, 19XX

Industrial County Human Resources Department
1335 N. 7th Street
Commerce City, XX 10101
(999) 555-6789

Completed proposals (including an original and three copies) must by physically in the possession of the Industrial County Human Resources Department at the address listed above prior to 4:30 p.m., July 14, 19XX.

TABLE OF CONTENTS

This request for Proposal (RFP) package contains all the information and forms necessary to complete and submit a proposal. Proposers are encouraged to review the Request for Proposal package in detail prior to commencing work.

SECTION I.   GENERAL INFORMATION

This Section represents a replication of the legal advertisement that appeared in the *Commerce City Times* on June 23, 19XX. Attention is directed to the following points:
  (A) The deadline for proposal submission.
  (B) The number of copies of the proposal to be submitted.
  (C) The designated contact person for questions concerning this Request for Proposal process.

SECTION II.   PROPOSAL REVIEW SCHEDULE

This Section outlines the schedule the Industrial County Human Resources Department intends to follow in issuing this Request for Proposals and in selecting contractors. The Department reserves the right to deviate from this schedule.

SECTION III.   PROPOSAL EVALUATION CRITERIA

This Section identifies the evaluation criteria to be used by the Department in reviewing all proposals submitted in response to this Request for Proposals.

SECTION IV.   WORK STATEMENT

This Section contains the homemaker work statement. Attention is directed to the requirement that homemaker contractors be licensed by the State Department of Health and Human Services.

SECTION V.   SERVICE DELIVERY HISTORY,
              KEY STAFF QUALIFICATIONS, FACILITIES
              AND EQUIPMENT

In this Section, proposers—using a narrative format—must detail and document their previous experience in providing homemaker services, must list the qualifications of key agency staff, and must describe facilities and equipment to be used.

SECTION VI.   PRICE QUOTES

This Section requires that proposers quote unit costs for all units of service provided. Proposers are cautioned that each unit price quoted for a given unit of service will be treated as a separate and distinct quote.

SECTION VIII.   PROPOSAL SUBMITTAL LETTER

This Section identifies all the portions of this Request for Proposals package that must be completed and returned and in the preferred order of sequence.

SECTION I
LEGAL ADVERTISEMENT

The Industrial County Human Resources Department hereby solicits proposals from qualified proposers to provide "Homemaker" services.

Request For Proposal packages may be obtained by writing:

> Industrial County Human Resources Department
> 1335 N. 7th Street
> Commerce City, XX 10101

or by calling (999) 555-6789.

Completed proposals, including an original and three (3) copies, must be physically in the possession of Industrial County Human Resources Department at the address listed above by 4:30 p.m. on Friday, July 14, 19XX.

A proposer's conference will be held at 1:00 p.m., Monday, June 30, 19XX in the Conference Room of the Industrial County Human Resources Department at which time any questions concerning the RFP package will be addressed. Proposers who do not attend the proposer's conference do so at their own risk. Questions concerning this Request for Proposals package should be addressed to Lawrence L. Martin at 555-6789 or by writing to the address noted above.

This announcement does not commit the Industrial County Human Resources Department to award a contract or to pay any costs incurred in the preparation of proposals. The Industrial County Human Resources Department reserves the right to accept or reject, in whole or in part, all proposals submitted and/or to cancel this announcement. All contracts awarded shall be based upon the proposal(s) most advantageous to the Industrial County Human Resources Department, price and other factors considered. All contracts are subject to the availability of funds and multiple contracts may be awarded.

SECTION II
PROPOSAL REVIEW SCHEDULE

Activity	Date
(1) Request for Proposals announced	June 23, 19XX
(2) Proposer's Conference (staff will respond to questions concerning the RFP)	June 28, 19XX
(3) Last day for proposers to submit proposals	July 14, 19XX
(4) Proposal Review Committee meets (proposers will be afforded 30 minutes each to make a brief presentation and to respond to questions from the Review Committee)	July 17, 19XX
(5) Contractor(s) announced—unsuccessful applicants notified by mail	August 1, 19XX
(6) Contract negotiations finalized	August 15, 19XX
(7) Contracts awarded	September 1, 19XX

The Industrial County Human Resources Department reserves the right to deviate from this schedule.

SECTION III
PROPOSAL EVALUATION CRITERIA

Criteria	Maximum Points
(1) Demonstrated Effectiveness	60
The demonstrated effectiveness of the proposer in providing homemaker services as evidenced by the organization's service delivery history and key staff qualifications.	
(2) Cost	40
The reasonableness of the quoted prices for the stated units of service.	
Maximum Points	100

SECTION IV
HOMEMAKER SERVICES WORK STATEMENT

SECTION V
SERVICE DELIVERY HISTORY &
KEY STAFF QUALIFICATIONS

In this Section, the proposer should document previous experience in the delivery of homemaker services including the names, titles, addresses, and telephone numbers of any federal, state, or local government agencies for which the proposer has previously provided such services. The names and resumés of key staff to be involved in the provision of service must also be included.

SECTION VI
PRICE QUOTES

Proposers are to quote their unit cost prices for providing given units of service in the spaces provided below. Only quotes appearing in the appropriate blank spaces on this page will be considered. Proposers may quote prices for any or all units of service.

For 1,000 units of homemaker service, a unit cost of $ _____
For 2,000 units of homemaker service, a unit cost of $ _____
For 3,000 units of homemaker service, a unit cost of $ _____

NOTE: A unit of homemaker service is defined as 60 minutes of service time.

SECTION VII
PROPOSAL SUBMITTAL LETTER

Mr. Lawrence Martin
Industrial County Human Resources Department
1335 N. 7th Street
Commerce, XX 10101

Dear Mr. Martin:

In response to your announcement dated June 23, 19XX, please accept this proposal.

I hereby certify that, to the best of my knowledge and belief, prices supplied in support of this proposal are accurate, complete, and current as of July 14, 19XX.

I additionally certify that I am duly authorized to submit this proposal on behalf of my organization.

Questions concerning this proposal should be addressed to _____
_____ at _____.
       (Name)   (Telephone)

Sincerely,

Signature _____   _____
       (Authorized Individual)   (Date)

Typed Name _____

Title _____

SECTION VIII
PROPOSAL SUBMITTAL CHECKLIST

(1) Proposal submittal letter
(2) Work statement
(3) Service delivery history and key staff qualifications
(4) Price quotes

References

American Bar Association. (1981). *The model procurement code for state and local governments.* Washington, DC: Author.

American Public Welfare Association. (1981). *Study of purchase of social services in selected states.* Washington, DC: Author.

Anthony, R. N., & Hertzlinger, R. (1975). Pricing. In *Management controls in nonprofit organizations.* Homewood, IL: Irwin.

Austin, M. J., and associates. (1982). *Evaluating your agency's programs.* Beverly Hills, CA: Sage.

Benton, B., Field, T., & Millar, R. (1978). *Social services: Federal legislation vs. state implementation.* Washington, DC: The Urban Institute.

Booz-Allen, & Hamilton. (1971). *Purchase of service: A study of the experiences of three states in purchase of service under the provision of the 1967 amendments to the social security act.* Washington, DC: Social & Rehabilitation Services, U.S. Dept. of Health, Education, and Welfare.

Born, C. E. (1983, March/April). Proprietary firms and child welfare services: Patterns and implications. *Child Welfare, 62,* 109-118.

Bowers, G. E., & Bowers, M. R. (1976). *The elusive unit of service.* Washington, DC: Project SHARE, Office of the Secretary, U.S. Department of Health, Education, and Welfare.

Buck, M. F. et al. (1973). *Developing contract work statements.* Columbus: Ohio State University Research Foundation.

Cohen, H. (1980). *You can negotiate anything.* New York: Bantam.

Cole, R. F. (1979, Summer). Social reform frustrated by bureaucratic routine: Title XX in Massachusetts. *Public Policy, 27,* 273-299.

Comptroller General of the United States. (1980). *Federal and state actions needed to overcome problems in administering the Title XX program.* Washington, DC: General Accounting Office.

Council of State Government. (1975). *State and local government purchasing.* Lexington: Author.

Daley, J., & Kettner, P. (1981). Bargaining in community development. *Journal of the Community Development Society, 12*(2), 25-38.

Demone, H. W., & Gibelman, M. (1984). *Purchasing human services: Policies, programs and procedures.* New York: Human Sciences Press.

Drucker, P. (1969). The sickness in government. In *The age of discontinuity.* New York: Harper & Row.

Elkin, R. (1980). *A human service manager's guide to developing unit costs.* Falls Church, VA: Institute for Information Studies.

Filley, A. C., House, R. J., & Kerr, S. (1976). *Managerial process and organizational behavior.* Glenview, IL: Scott, Foresman.

Fisher, R., & Ury, W. (1981). *Getting to yes. Negotiating agreement without giving in.* Boston: Houghton Mifflin.

Fisk, D., Kiesling, H., & Muller, T. (1978). *Private provision of public services—an overview.* Washington, DC: The Urban Institute.

Florestano, P. S., & Gordon, S. B. (1980, January/February). Public vs. private: Small government contracting with the private section. *Public Administration Review, 1,* 29-34.

Franklin, D. S., & White, M. (1975). *Contracting for purchase of services: A procedural manual.* Los Angeles: Regional Research Institute in Social Welfare, School of Social Work, University of Southern California.

General Services Administration. (n.d.). *Government contract administration.* Washington, DC: Federal Supply Service, General Services Administration.

General Services Administration. (n.d.). *Contracting by formal advertising.* Washington, DC: Federal Supply Service, General Services Administration.

Ghere, R. K. (1981, Spring). Effects of service delivery variations on administration of municipal human services agencies: The contract approach versus agency implementation. *Administration in Social Work, 5,* 65-78.

Gibelman, M., & Demone, H. W., Jr. (1983, Winter). Purchase of service: Forgoing public-private partnerships in human services. *The Urban and Social Change Review, 16,* 21-26.

Gurin, A., et al. (1980). *Contracting for services as a mechanism for the delivery of human services: A study of contracting practices in three human service agencies in Massachusetts.* Waltham, MA: Brandeis University-Florence Heller Graduate School for Advanced Studies in Social Welfare.

Hatry, H., & Valente, C. F. (1983). Alternative service delivery approaches involving increased use of the private sector. *The Municipal Year Book—1983.* Washington, DC: International City Management Association.

Jansson, B. S. (1979, May). Public monitoring of contracts with nonprofit organizations: Organizational mission in two sectors. *Journal of Sociology and Social Welfare, 6,* 362-374.

Kahn, A. (1978). The impact of purchase of service contracting on social service delivery. In K. R. Wedel, A. J. Katz, & A. Weick (Eds.), *Proceedings of the National Institute on purchase of service contracting.* Lawrence: University of Kansas, School of Social Work.

Kelley, J. T. (1984). *Costing government services: A guide for decision making.* Washington, DC: Government Finance Officers Association.

Kettner, P. M., Daley, J. M., & Nichols, A. W. (1985). *Initiating change in organizations and communities.* Monterey, CA: Brooks/Cole.

Kettner, P. M., & Martin, L. L. (1985a). Generating competition in the human services through purchase of service contracting. In D. L. Thompson (Ed.), *The private exercise of public functions.* Port Washington: Associated Faculty Press.

Kettner, P. M., & Martin, L. L. (1985b, Fall). Issues in the development of monitoring systems for purchase of service contracting. *Administration in Social Work, 9,* 69-82.

Kramer, R. M. (1966, March). Voluntary agencies and the use of public funds: Some policy issues. *Social Service Review, 53,* 1-14.

Lauffer, A. (1984). *Grantsmanship* (2nd edition). Beverly Hills, CA: Sage.

Levin, E. (1980). *Negotiating tactics: Bargain your way to winning.* New York: Fawcett Columbine.

Lourie, N. V. (1978). Purchase of service contracting: Issues confronting the government sponsored agency. In K. R. Wedel, A. J. Katz, & A. Weick (Eds.), *Proceedings of the national institute on purchase of service contracting.* Lawrence: University of Kansas, School of Social Work.

Martin, L. L. (1986). *Purchase of service contracting in human services: an analysis of state decision making.* Dissertation, Arizona State University.

Massachusetts Taxpayers Foundation. (1980). *Purchase of service: Can state government gain control?* Boston: Author.

Mueller, C. P. (1978). Purchase of service contracting from the viewpoint of the provider. In K. R. Wedel, A. J. Katz, & A. Weick (Eds.), *Proceedings of the national institute on purchase of service contracting.* Lawrence: University of Kansas, School of Social Work.

Mueller, C. P. (1980, November/December). Five years later—a look at Title XX: The federal billion dollar social services fund. *Grantsmanship Center News, 8,* 27-37, 56-68.

National Aeronautics and Space Administration. (1974). *Guide for monitoring contractors' indirect cost.* Washington, DC: Author.

National Alliance of Business. (n.d.). *JOBS entry program.* Washington, DC: Manpower Administration, Department of Labor.

Nelson, B. J. (1980). Purchase of service. In J. Washnis (Ed.), *Productivity improvement handbook for state and local government.* New York: John Wiley.

Nierenberg, G. I. (1973). *Fundamentals of negotiating.* New York: Hawthorn.

Office of Federal Procurement Policy. (1979). *Principles of government contract law.* Washington, DC: Government Printing Office.

Office of Federal Procurement Policy. (1980). *Desk guide to price and cost analysis.* Washington, DC: Government Printing Office.

Pacific Consultants. (1979). *Title XX Purchase of Service: A description of states' service delivery and management practices.* Washington, DC: Administration for Public Service, U.S. Department of Health, Education, and Welfare.

Project IN-STEP. (1975). *How-to-do-it handbook, Volume V: Contracting, monitoring, evaluation.* Tallahassee: Project IN-STEP. Division of Aging, Florida Department of Health and Rehabilitation Services.

Richardson, D. R. (1981). *Rate setting in the human services: A guide for administrators.* Washington, DC: Project SHARE, Office of the Assistant Secretary for Planning and Evaluation, U.S. Department of Health and Human Services.

Rutter, L. (1981, June). Strategies for the essential community: Local government in the year 2000. *The Futurist, 15,* 19-28.

Sammet, G. J., & Kelley, C. G. (1981). *Subcontract management handbook.* New York: American Management Association.

Schatzki, M. (1981). *Negotiation. The art of getting what you want.* New York: New American Library.

Sharkansky, I. (1980, March/April). Policy making and service delivery on the margins of government: The case of contractors. *Public Administration Review, 40,* 116-123.

Simpson, L. P. (1965). *Handbook of the law of contracts.* St. Paul, MN: West.

Smith, B.L.R. (1973). Accountability and independence in the contract state. In B.L.R. Smith & D. C. Hague (Eds.), *The dilemma of accountability in modern government: Independence versus control.* New York: Macmillian.

Suchman, E. A. (1967). *Evaluative research.* New York: Russell Sage Foundation.

Teague, G. V. (1981, March). Request for a proposal: Solicitation for a federal contract. *Grants Magazine, 4,* 16-28.

Terrell, P. (1979, March). Private alternatives to public human services. *Social Service Review, 53,* 46-74.

U.S. Department of Commerce. (1979). *Control services handbook: Issues & impacts for the park and recreation manager.* Washington, DC: Heritage Conservation and Recreation Service, Author.

U.S. Department of Health, Education, and Welfare. (1971). *The negotiated contracting process.* Washington, DC: Author.

U.S. Department of Health, Education, and Welfare. (1976). *Cost principles and procedures for establishing cost allocation plans and indirect cost rates for grants and contracts with the federal government.* Washington, DC: Government Printing Office.

U.S. General Accounting Office. (1980). *Government contract principles.* Washington, DC: Government Printing Office.

United Way of America. (1976). UWASIS II: *A taxonomy of social goals and human services programs.* Alexandria, VA: United Way of America.

Warschaw, T. A. (1980). *Winning by negotiation.* New York: Berkley Books.

Wedel, K. R. (1973). *Government contracting for social services: Purchase of service in states' public assistance programs.* Dissertation, University of Pittsburg.

Wedel, K. R. (1974, Winter). Contracting for public assistance social services. *Public Welfare, 32,* 57-62.

Wedel, K. R. (1976, March). Government contracting for purchase of service. *Social Work, 21,* 101-105.

Wedel, K. R. (1983). Purchase of service. In R. Agranoff (Ed.), *Human services on a limited budget.* Washington, DC: International City Management Association.

Wedel, K. R., Katz, A. J., & Weick, A. (1979). *Social services by government contract: A policy analysis.* New York: Praeger.

Wickenden, E. (1976). Purchase of care and services: Effect on voluntary agencies. In N. Gilbert & H. Specht (Eds.), *The emergence of social welfare and social work.* Itasca: F. E. Peacock.

Winogrond, I. R. (1970). *Purchase of care and services in the health and welfare fields: Proceedings of the first Milwaukee Institute on a social welfare issue of the day.* Milwaukee: University of Wisconsin—Milwaukee School of Social Work.

About the Authors

PETER M. KETTNER, DSW, is an Associate Professor of Social Work at Arizona State University. He is author of two books and over twenty book chapters, journal articles, reports, and monographs. He has served as a consultant to state departments of social services in three states and has provided consultation and training to many private, nonprofit social service agencies. His areas of expertise include human services planning, social service agency administration, and purchase of service contracting.

LAWRENCE L. MARTIN, Ph.D., is Director of Management Analysis for Maricopa County (Phoenix) Arizona. He previously served as state Director of Aging Services for Arizona and Deputy Director of the Maricopa County Human Resources Department. He has provided consultation and training to many state, county, city, and private nonprofit social service agencies across the nation. He recently completed a national study and published several articles on purchase of service contracting in human services and has also conducted research and published extensively on the topic of transportation as it relates to the delivery of human services.

NOTES

NOTES

NOTES

NOTES

NOTES